Inga Ettelt, Silvia Koch, Nicole Malik, Kevin Marc Patterson, Stefanie Phlippen, Anne Sutter

Herausgeberin: Sandra Deneke

navi
Englisch 7/8

1. Auflage, 1. korrigierter Nachdruck 2014

Bestellnummer 61282

Bildungsverlag EINS

Diese Zeichen findest du in diesem Buch

Diese Zeichen bei den Aufgaben sagen dir, was du tun könntest:

 Hört das Tonbeispiel an

 Schreibe in dein Heft

 Arbeite mit einem Partner oder einer Partnerin

AH Weitere Aufgaben im Arbeitsheft

 Beschaffe dir Informationen

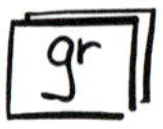

Hier hilft dir die Grammatik-Seite weiter

Achtung! Hier musst du aufpassen

Diese Zeichen am unteren Rand sagen dir etwas zum Lernbereich:

Hören und Verstehen

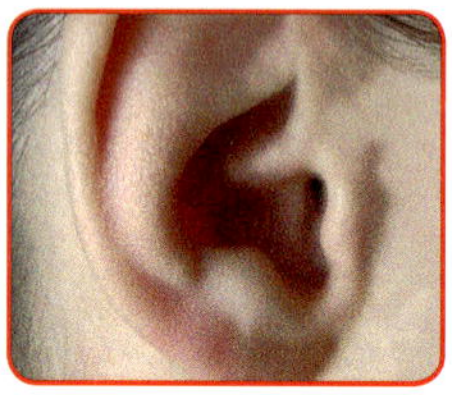

Sprechen

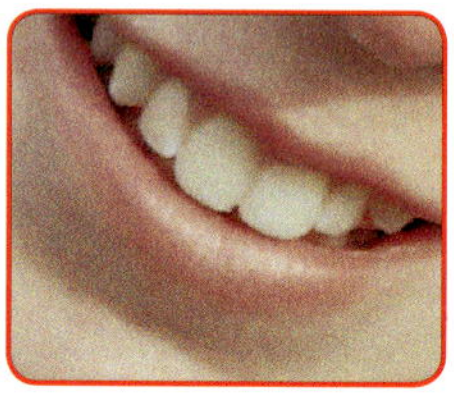

Schreiben

Mit Texten arbeiten

Wortschatz erweitern

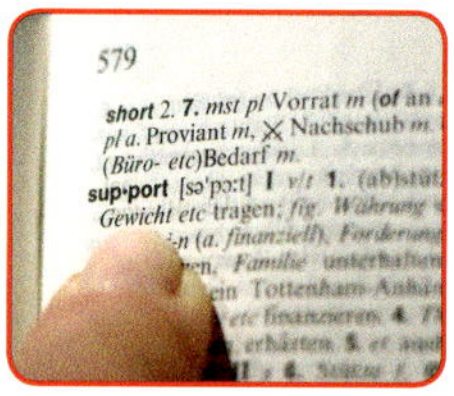

Mit Sprache richtig umgehen

Hinweis: Die Nummerierung der Audio-Tracks basiert auf der Reihenfolge der Schülerbuchseiten und ihrer entsprechenden Arbeitsheftseiten.

www.diesterweg.de

Bildungshaus Schulbuchverlage
Georg-Westermann-Allee 66, 38104 Braunschweig

ISBN 978-3-427-**61282**-7

Contents

1	**Welcome back to English: I am good at English**	6	
	Do you remember?	8	Bildbeschreibungen verstehen
	Best friends	9	einem Text Informationen entnehmen
	Collecting information	10	ein Interview führen
	Make your own book of school friends	11	über sich selbst Auskunft geben
2	**About me: My best friend**	12	
	What best friends do together	14	sich über Freundschaften austauschen
	My best friend	15	einen Hörtext zum Thema Freundschaft verstehen
	What a best friend should be like	16	Vorlieben äußern
	Different types of best friends	17	Typbeschreibungen verstehen
	Strategy: Making a word list	18	
	Poems about the best friend	19	ein eigenes Gedicht schreiben und gestalten
	Dialogue between two friends	20	einen Dialog spielen
	This is what you have learned	21	
3	**At school: At the cafeteria**	22	
	What do you want to eat?	24	Essen bestellen
	What is on the menu?	25	aus einer Speisekarte auswählen
	Making a sandwich	26	Vorlieben ausdrücken
	Why the sandwich is called sandwich	27	Informationen aus einfachen Sachtexten entnehmen
	Baked potatoes recipe	28	Rezepte lesen und verstehen
	Healthy food	30	über ein Thema diskutieren
	Helping a friend	31	über ein Thema diskutieren
	Strategy: Word pictures	32	
	This is what you have learned	33	
4	**Free time: A fancy dress party**	34	
	Paul's fancy dress party	36	Bildergeschichten verstehen
	Strategy: Writing an invitation card	38	
	My favourite singer	39	sich über ein Thema austauschen
	Recipes: Making a trifle	40	Rezepte lesen
	Morning star cocktail	41	Rezepte schreiben
	Let's dance	42	Handlungsanweisungen verstehen und befolgen
	This is what you have learned	43	

Contents

5	**My body: At the doctor's**	44	
	Emily is ill	46	einem Text Informationen über das Wohlbefinden entnehmen
	At the doctor's	48	ein Gespräch mit einem Arzt verstehen
	I feel very ill	49	ein Gespräch mit einem Arzt führen
	You're lucky!	50	Internetchats verstehen
	Web page "The flu"	51	einen Sachtext zum Thema Krankheiten verstehen
	Strategy: Word clusters	52	
	This is what you have learned	53	
6	**The world of work: Money and jobs**	54	
	Window-shopping	56	einen Dialog verstehen
	Talking about pocket money	58	sich über das Thema Taschengeld austauschen
	Jobs for teens	59	Jobvorschläge machen
	You could, but would you?	60	Jobvorschläge abwägen
	Would you like the job?	61	Argumente für und wider finden
	Strategy: pros and cons	62	
	Planning a flea market	63	Ideen sammeln
	At the flea market	64	Verkaufsdialoge führen
	This is what you have learned	65	
7	**Around the house: Energy**	66	
	Things we use	68	Pro und Contra einander gegenüberstellen
	Energy is limited	69	Textinhalte mit eigenen Worten wiedergeben
	Electricity is everywhere!	70	Wortschatz zum Thema Haushalt erweitern
	The use of electricity	71	über Elektrizität sprechen
	There is a lot of electricity in a house	72	eine Handlungsanweisung erstellen und ausführen
	The shoe box house	73	eine Handlungsanweisung lesen und umsetzen
	Strategy: Mind map	74	
	This is what you have learned	75	

8	**Around town: The class trip**	76	
	Where would you like to go?	78	Informationen sammeln und präsentieren
	The information-poster	79	eine Handlungsanweisung lesen und umsetzen
	Places to visit in London	80	verschiedenen Medien Informationen entnehmen
	Things to know about London	81	ein Thema präsentieren
	How to get around London	82	über Landeskunde sprechen
	Strategy: On the tube in London	83	
	A musical digression: "Streets of London"	84	den Text eines Liedes hören und verstehen
	This is what you have learned	85	
9	**Around the world: The news**	86	
	What do daily news consist of?	88	einem Text Informationen entnehmen
	The categories of daily news	89	Kategorien bilden
	Why news is so important	90	einen Text anhören und verstehen
	The legend of Finn Mac Cool	91	über Landeskunde sprechen
	Different themes – different tenses	92	eine Schlagzeile zeitlich einordnen
	Strategy: Different tenses – different meaning	93	
	A musical digression: "A day in the life"	94	ein Lied hören und verstehen
	This is what you have learned	95	
10	**Around the year: Holidays**	96	
	Who is your Valentine?	98	Entscheidungsfragen stellen
	I love you	100	Gefühle ausdrücken
	The first Thanksgiving	101	einem Text landeskundliche Informationen entnehmen
	A Thanksgiving Dinner	102	Vorlieben und Abneigungen ausdrücken
	The story of Rosa Parks	103	Geschichten verstehen
	About Martin Luther King Day	105	landeskundliche Informationen verstehen
	Strategy: Looking for information	106	
	This is what you have learned	107	
11	**Grammar: To play with language**	108	Grammatik
	Dictionary	130	
	In English, please!	149	
	Texts	151	

1 Welcome back to English:

I am good at English

1 Welcome back to English:

Do you remember?

Track 01

Before you listen to the text:

1. Look at the pictures on pages 6 and 7.
2. Which one do **you** remember?
3. Note down some words and describe the picture to your class.

While you listen to the text:

4. Point to the picture that Paul and Emily are talking about.

AH

After you have listened to the text:

5. There is one picture Paul and Emily do not talk about. Find it, make notes and then tell your class about it.

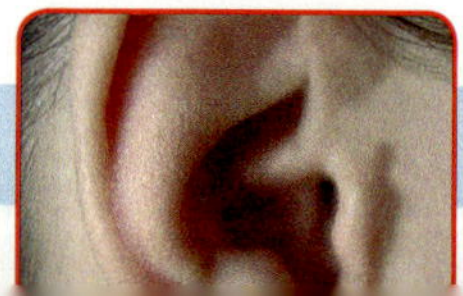

Best friends

Track 02

Emily Jones is now 13 years old. She lives in Bristol with her mother and her brother Robert. They have also got a dog. They live in a flat. She's got a lot of friends: her best friend Paul Morris, Tanja from Germany and Carla, a girl from school. Emily likes sports: she plays table tennis, beach volleyball and she goes inline skating. Her favourite subjects are science and English. She loves ice cream.

Paul Morris is now 14 years old. He lives in Bristol with his parents and his sister Sarah. They have got a cat. Paul loves all animals. Paul's family lives in a nice house and he has got a nice room. On the wall there are posters of pop stars. He loves to listen to music. Together with Emily he does a lot of sports. But he also likes to play computer games and to chat with friends. His favourite subjects are music and IT.

AH

1. Who is it?
   - Who has got a cat?
   - Who likes sports?
   - Who has got a brother?
   - Who loves to listen to music?
   - Who likes English at school?
   - Who lives in a nice house?
2. Ask your class more questions about Emily and Paul.
3. Make two lists and note down all the information you can get about Paul and Emily.

Emily	Paul
• *13 years old*	• *14 years old*

Collecting information

1. Choose a partner for an interview. Find out as much about him or her as you can.

Track 04

Here are some questions you can ask:

AH

2. Note down the answers. Then tell your class about the person.

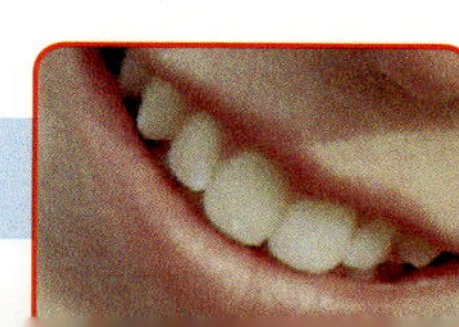

Make your own book of school friends

1. Write a short text about yourself.
   Use the questions on page 10 or the texts about Emily and Paul on page 9.

You need:
- a sheet of A4-sized paper
- a needle
- thread
- scissors

Fold your paper in half.

↓

Fold the paper in half again.

↓

Sew along the long side of the paper.

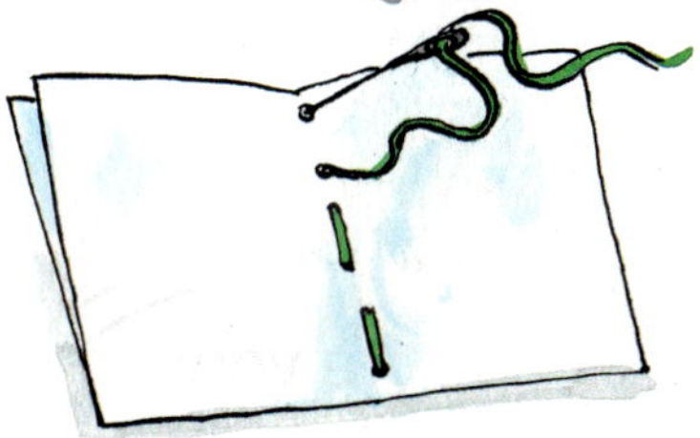

↓

Cut open the short sides of the paper.

2. In this book you can collect the texts of all your friends.
   Write **your** text into the books of your friends.
   Glue the book of friends into your “me-book” if you want.

2 About me:

Track 05

My best friend

What best friends do together

AH

Emily and Carla have secrets together.

Paul and Cem …

Lilly and Susan ….

Linda and Sarah ….

Jim and John ….

Tom and Marc ….

Mary and Steven …

Robin and Sue ….

Emily and Carla

Paul and Cem

Lilly and Susan

Linda and Sarah

Tom and Marc

Robin and Sue

Steven and Mary

Jim and John

1. What do best friends do together?
2. Look at the pictures. Say the sentences.
3. What do **you** and **your** best friend do together? Look at the sentences below.
4. Talk about it in class.

<table>
<tr><td>We</td><td>play computer games
relax in the park
go shopping</td><td>together.</td></tr>
</table>

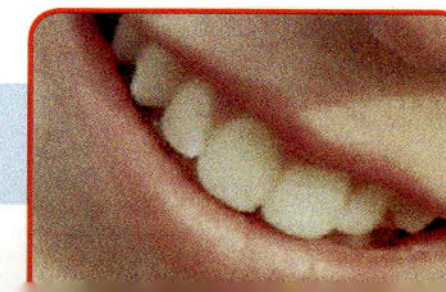

My best friend

Track 07

AH

Hi. My name is Emily. I have a best friend. Her name is Carla. We see each other at school. And we meet each other almost every evening. Or we talk on the phone. We talk a lot about our friends, about our families, about style and … well, that's a secret. We have a lot of secrets. That's what friends are for.

Hi. My name is Paul. I have a best friend, too. His name is Cem. He's my neighbour. We see each other after school every day. We play football or basketball together. On Fridays we go to the youth club and play table football or billiards. Sometimes we fight but the next day we're friends again.

1. What about **you**? Do **you** have secrets with **your** best friend? Do **you** fight with **your** best friend? Discuss in class.

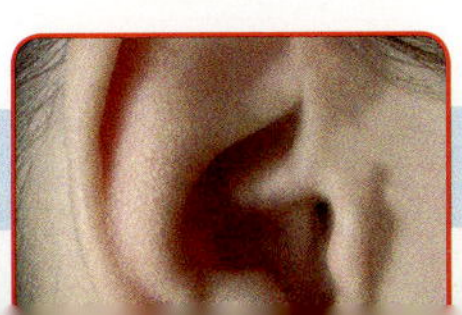

What a best friend should be like

Track 08

AH

What about **your** best friend? What **should** he/she be like?
Say statements like this:

My best friend	should	like music. play hockey. have money. help me. care about me. like to party. look good.

1. Talk about friendship with a partner.
2. Think of other things a best friend should be or should do.
3. Make a list. Talk about it in class.

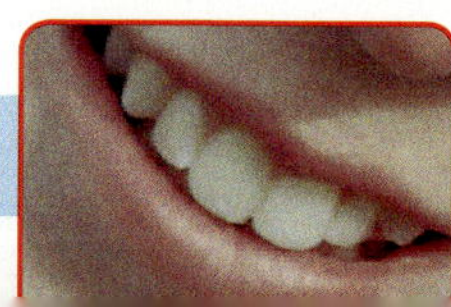

Different types of best friends

Listen and read.

Track 09

Type A
You're a really good friend.
You're a friend in good and in bad times.
You take care of your friends.
Everybody should have a friend like you.

Type B
You're a superficial friend.
Money and looks are more important to you than character.
You're not ready to be a best friend, yet.
Work on it.

Type C
You're a fun-orientated friend.
You want to enjoy the friendship.
You want to **do** things with your friend.
You don't like to talk or to listen to problems.
Be careful that you don't lose your best friend.

1. What type of friend are **you**? What do you think?
2. Check with the test in your workbook 7.

AH

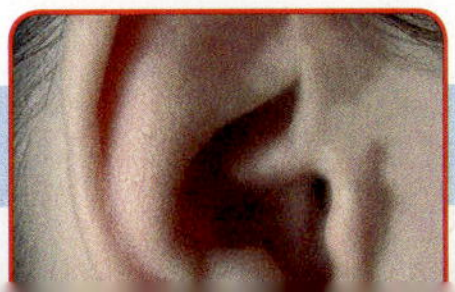

Strategy:

Making a word list

A word list helps you to express yourself on a certain subject.

1.
Take a sheet of A4-sized paper and felt-tips.

2.
Write down the title of the subject in the middle of the paper.

3.
Think of words that go with the subject.

4.
Write the words down.
Look up words you don't know in English in the dictionary.

AH

5.
Now make an ABC-list like this:

adjectives

a	arrogant – arrogant
b	big – groß
c	cool – cool, kühl
d	
e	
f	
g	

6.
If you have two words with the same letter, order the words alphabetically.

Poems about the best friend

Track 10

a) You are incredible, that's what you are,
you are funny, you are a star.
You are friendly to me,
you hang out together with me.
You are beautiful, what a dream,
my best friend, we are such a perfect team.

b) If you were a colour, you'd be bright red.
If you were an animal, you'd be wild.
If you were a car, you'd be fast.
If you were music, you'd be loud.
You're all this, bright red, wild, fast and loud,
but what's best: you are my friend!

c)
ELEGANT
SMART
NICE
LOVELY
SILLY

1. Read the three poems and listen to them on CD.
2. Make an ABC-list with the title adjectives (look at page 18).
3. Write your own poem. Replace all the red words in the poems with your own words. The list can help you. Choose a different activity for the verb in green.
4. Illustrate your poem and present it to the class.

AH

ein eigenes Gedicht schreiben und gestalten

Dialogue between two friends

Track 11

Cem: “OK, then let's play billiards together.”

Paul: “Oh no, not again.”

Cem: “Alright, let's play basketball, then.”

Paul: “I don't want to play basketball.”

Cem: “What's wrong with you?”

Paul: “Let's walk in the park.”

Cem: “Let's **what**? Why walk in the park? What for?”

Paul: “Let's just hang out.”

Cem: “I don't want to just hang out.”

Paul: “Let's relax, sit on a bench.”

Cem: “I don't want to sit around. I want to **do** something.”

Paul: “Alright, you play basketball and I … watch the girls.”

AH

1. Read the text. Listen to the dialogue on CD. Act it out.
2. Write your own dialogue. Work with a partner.
3. Act the scene.

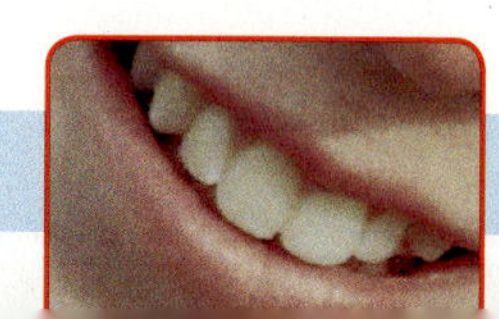

This is what you have learned

Walk from field to field and collect **5 points per answer**.
If you are not sure, look it up and try again.

start

What should your best friend be like?

What do you do when your best friend is sad?

Name five adjectives.

What do these best friends do together?

You want to do something with your best friend. What do you say?

What do you and your best friend do together?

Name an adjective that begins with the letter "s".

What do these best friends do together?

Your friend tells you: "Let's play basketball."

What do you answer?

What do these best friends do together?

Name an adjective that begins with the letter "b".

finish

Results:
55 points = Congratulations!
40 points and more = Good!
15 points and more = Have a look at the chapter again.
Less than 15 points = What did you do? Sleep? ☺

3 At school:

Track 13

AH

At the cafeteria

What do you want to eat?

Track 14

1. What do you want to eat? Say: *I want to eat ...*
2. Work in pairs. Prepare the scene and act it. One of you is the pupil. You must order the food. Say: *I would like ...* The other one is the cafeteria staff person: Ask your partner what he or she wants to eat.

AH

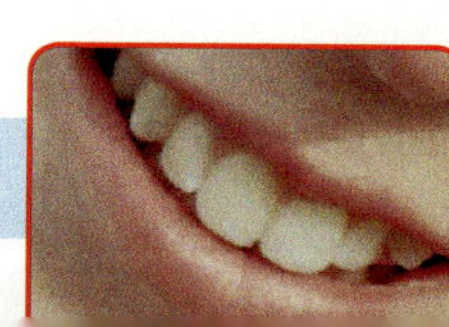

What is on the menu?

MENU

Monday	hamburger on bun French fries salad peaches
Tuesday	pizza peas and carrots pears
Wednesday	chili with crackers bread and butter celery stick chocolate pudding
Thursday	chicken nuggets mashed potato and gravy corn applesauce
Friday	cheese or ham sandwich ravioli in sauce fruit cocktail

AH

1. Read the menu. What is on the menu? Are there words you do not know?
2. What would you eat? Say: *I would … .*
3. Do you like the menu? Write your own menu for a school cafeteria. If you do not know a word, look it up in the dictionary.

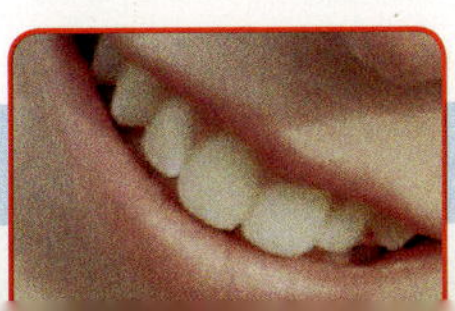

Making a sandwich

Track 15

Emily: "What have you got for lunch today?"
Paul: "I've got a sandwich."
Emily: "Oh me too. I don't like the menu today.
What's on your sandwich?"
Paul: "Ham and egg. What about yours?"
Emily: "I've got lettuce and cheese on my sandwich.
Do you want to swap?"
Paul: "Yes I do, let's swap."

How to make a sandwich:

1. Read the dialogue in pairs.
2. Do your parents give you a sandwich for lunch? What is on it?
3. What is on your perfect sandwich?
   Tell the class. Say: *On my perfect sandwich ...*

AH

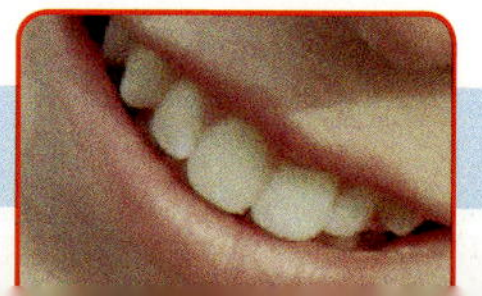

Why the sandwich is called sandwich

Track 17

Sandwich is a town in the south of England. But the sandwich is probably named after the 4th Earl of Sandwich. He lived in the 18th century (1718–1792). His name was John Montagu. He really liked to play cards.

Sometimes he played for 24 hours. He did not even stop for dinner. So he asked his servant to bring him roast beef between two slices of bread. Now he could play and eat, because his fingers stayed clean.

That is how Lord Sandwich invented the sandwich.

1. Read the text.
2. Find the town of Sandwich in the map.
3. Find out more about John Montagu on the internet. Present it to class.

Baked potatoes recipe

For 5 persons you need:
- 5 big potatoes
- aluminium foil

Toppings:
- 100 g butter
- 200 g sour cream
- 3 tomatoes
- 2 sweet peppers
- 3 spring onions
- 50 g bacon
- 100 g ham
- 200 g cheddar cheese
- 50 g parmesan cheese
- salt and pepper

This is what you need to do:

Wash the potatoes, put aluminium foil around them. Make some little holes with a fork.

Bake them for about 45 minutes at 180 °C. Put the butter and sour cream on plates. Cut the tomatoes, the spring onions, the sweet peppers, the bacon and the ham in little pieces.

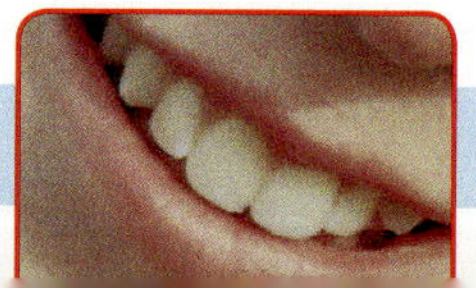

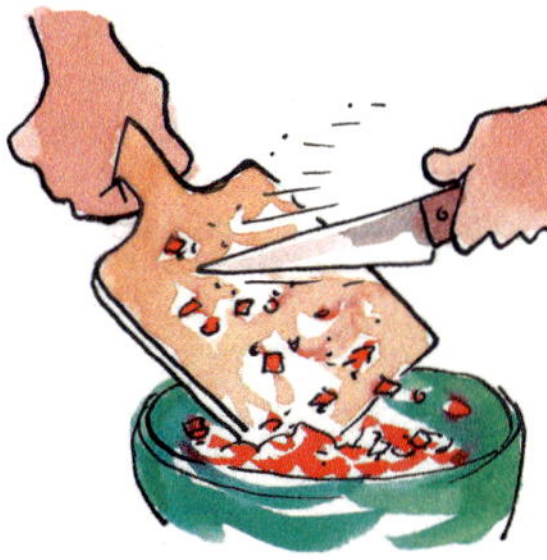

Put them in bowls. Grate the cheddar cheese and the parmesan cheese and put it in bowls. Set the table.

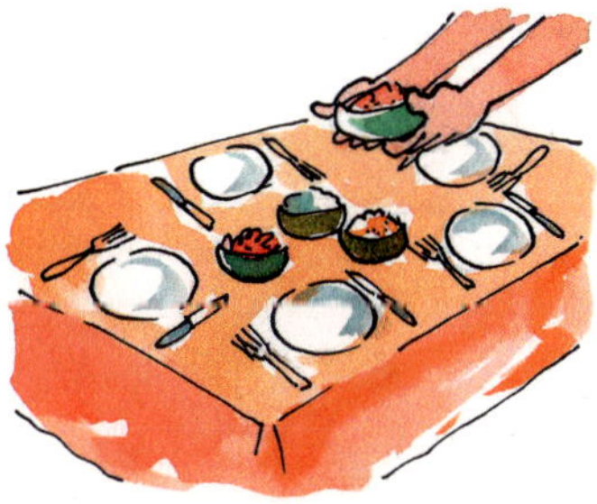

Place the bowls and plates with the toppings in the middle of the table. Everyone takes a baked potato and puts it on his or her plate. Take a knife and make a long, deep cut on top of the potato.

Put some salt and pepper over your potato. Take any topping you like and put it in the cut.

1. Make baked potatoes in your school kitchen.

Healthy food

Track 18

Paul and Emily are in class. They talk about healthy food. The teacher draws a big mind map on the board.
The teacher asks: "What do you think healthy food is?"
Emily answers: "Salad is healthy. There are lots of vitamins in it."
"That's right," the teacher says, "very good Emily."
Paul whispers: "I don't think hamburger with chips are very healthy."
The teacher smiles: "That's right, Paul."

1. Make a mind map with healthy food in class.
2. Look at the menu on page 25 (or the menu you wrote). Is that healthy food?
3. What do you eat in a day? Talk about it in class. What can you do to make it healthier?

AH

4. Paul says: *I want to eat healthy food. So I can never eat sweets again.*
   Is he right?

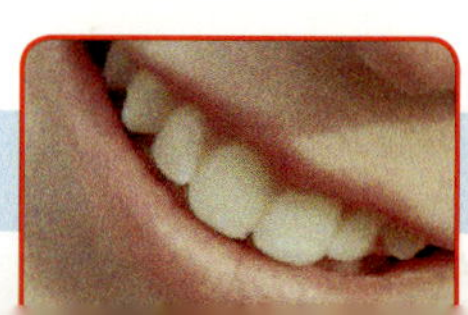

Helping a friend

Paul's friend James is sad.
He thinks he is too fat.
Other children laugh at him.

Paul wants to help him.
He tells him what he learned in school about healthy food.

They make a list together:

James:	
breakfast:	*pancakes, bacon and egg roll, hot chocolate*
lunch:	*hamburger on bun, French fries, cookies, Coke*
dinner:	*mashed potatoes, sausages and gravy, ice cream*
in between:	*chocolate, cake, cookies, pudding, chips*

1. What is wrong about James' eating habits? Discuss in class.
2. Changing the eating habits is not easy. How can James start?
3. What else can he do to improve his health?
   Write your ideas in your excercise book.

AH

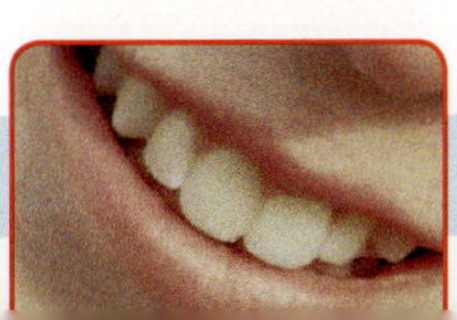

Strategy:

Sometimes it's hard to find a word picture. Be creative, it only has to help you. Not everybody has to understand it!

Word pictures

It is easier to remember words in **word pictures**:
Try it like this:

Cheese +  = 

Mix the written word and the meaning of it in a **word picture**. Write a vocabulary list like this:

English	word picture	German
cheese		Käse

It is not only possible with nouns, you can also make pictures of verbs and adjectives:

to look		sehen, schauen
tall		groß, hoch

There are many different ways to make word pictures:

a) Mix the letters and the meaning:  or ,

b) Make a picture with some of the letters: 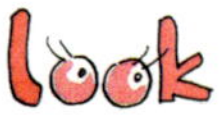 or ,

c) Write the word in a special way or form: ,

d) Put a picture next to or on top of the word: , ,

e) Write the word into the picure: ,

f) … or whatever comes to your mind.

1. Make word pictures with "small" and "football".
2. Choose some words from the vocabulary list at the end of the book and make word pictures. Present the best one to your class.

This is what you have learned

Let's play a game

Pupil 1 starts:

I want a pizza with CHEESE. What do you want?

Pupil 2 answers:

I want a pizza with cheese and TOMATOES. What do you want?

Then Pupil 3 answers:

I want a pizza with cheese, tomatoes and HAM. What do you want?

and so on ...

Always repeat what the pupils before you wanted (*I want a pizza with xxx, xxx, xxx ...*) and then add something (*... and xxx*). Try to remember everything or let your classmates help you. Then ask the next pupil: What do you want?

- *You can also play it with:*
- *I want a sandwich with ...* *What do you want?*
- *I want a baked potato with ...* *What do you want?*
- *...*

4 Free time:

Track 19

AH

A fancy dress party

Paul's fancy dress party

Track 20

Paul is preparing a fancy dress party. Here you can see him writing invitation cards for his friends.

At school, he's giving the invitation cards to Emily, Rob, Claire, Tom and Betty.

The next day, Emily and Claire are making plans for Paul's party.

Paul is in the kitchen. He's preparing some snacks and drinks for his party. His mum is helping him.

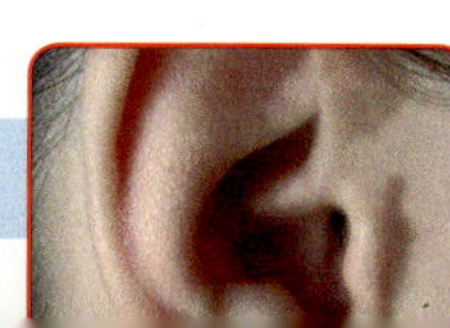

Paul's dad is in the living room. He's helping with the decorations.

It's Saturday and it's party time! The friends are on their way to Paul's house.

The friends are enjoying the snacks and drinks at Paul's party. Suddenly, Paul remembers something.

1. Read and listen to the text.
2. What is going to happen next? Take a camera and take photos or draw pictures.
3. Present your story to the class.

Strategy:

Writing an invitation card

This is Paul's invitation card:

Dear Emily,

please come to my fancy dress party!

When: *on Saturday, the 15th May*
Time: *at four o'clock*
Where: *at 76 Park Road, Bristol*

Please tell me if you can come.

Your friend Paul

AH

1. Make your own invitation cards. Remember to tell your guests **where** the party is and **when** it starts.

My favourite singer

If you want to have a party, you'll need good music.

Paul has made a poster:

Madonna

Birthday: 16th August 1958
Hobbies: yoga,
writing books
music
Songs: *4 minutes*
Hung up
Give it 2 me
and many more

1. Who is **your** favourite singer? Tell the class.
2. Make a poster about **your** favourite singer and present it to the class.

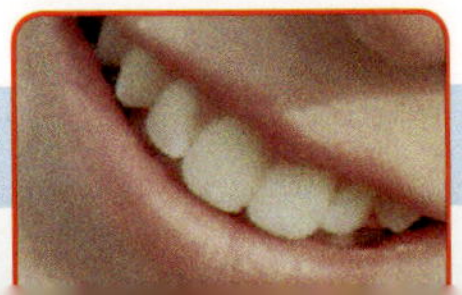

Recipes: Making a trifle

You need (for ten people):

- 24 ladyfingers
- 100 ml of orange juice
- different kinds of fruit
- ready-made custard
- whipped cream

a) Place the ladyfingers in a bowl.

b) Pour orange juice over them.

c) Peel and slice the fruit.

d) Decorate the fruit on top of the ladyfingers.

e) Spoon the custard onto the fruit.

f) Cover the custard with whipped cream.

g) Enjoy it!

1. Make a trifle together with your class.

Morning star cocktail

You need (for three people):

- 1 teaspoon sugar
- 1 teaspoon honey
- 300 ml pineapple juice
- 300 ml mineral water
- vanilla sugar
- 3 pineapple chunks

Mix everything and pour it in three glasses. Decorate every glass with a pineapple chunk.

1. Make the cocktail together with your class.
2. Do you know another cocktail? Look up recipes on the internet or write a new recipe.
3. Make the cocktails together with your class.

Let's dance

Track 22

Paul wants to learn a new dance for his party. He asks Emily to help him.

Paul: "Show me a dance, please."
Emily: "Take one step forward. Take two steps to the right. You're doing really well!"
Paul: "Do you really think so?"
Emily: "Yes. Now, turn around and clap your hands twice. Take two steps backward and one step to the left. Bend your knees. Stand up again. Claire will be impressed!"
Paul: "Thank you for teaching me, Emily."

1. Read the text.
2. Do you know any other dances? Write down the instructions.

This is what you have learned

We're having a party

Prepare a party for your school/your class/another class … .

- What kind of party are you going to plan?
- Write invitation cards.
- Which music are you going to play?
- Prepare English snacks and drinks.
- Practise a dance and show it to your guests.
- Take pictures of the preparations and of your party. Make a poster.

5 My body:

Track 23

AH

At the doctor's

Emily is ill

Track 24

It's Monday morning. Emily and her mother are in the kitchen. Emily's mother is making breakfast.

Emily: "Mum, I feel very ill today."
Mum: "What's the problem?"
Emily: "I've got a sore throat. I think I've got a cold."
Mum: "Yes, you don't look well. Have you got a fever?"
Emily: "I don't know. Where's the thermometer?"
Mum: "I'll get it. Drink a cup of tea with honey, dear!"

Emily: "Mum, it's 38.5 °C."
Mum: "Well, then, back to bed with you. You shouldn't go to school. But you must see a doctor."
Emily: "But … we'll write an English test today."
Mum: "No, you stay at home. I'll make you some fresh orange juice and then I'll call Doctor McMillan."

Receptionist: "Dr. McMillan's surgery. Can I help you?"

Mum: "Yes. My daughter Emily is ill. She's got a cold and a fever. I think she needs to see the doctor. Can she come today?"

Receptionist: "One moment, let me check. Yes, she can come at 11.15. But maybe she must wait a little."

Mum: "That's OK. I'll send her."

1. **Before** reading the text:
   Look at the pictures. What is the story about? Describe the pictures.
2. Find all the words from the word field "doctor" (e.g. *ill, sore throat, surgery ...*). Write them on cards and put them up on the wall.
3. Read the sentences. They are not correct.
   Can you correct them?

AH

- Emily has got a stomach ache.
- Emily drinks a cup of tea.
- Emily hasn't got a fever.
- Emily will write a maths test today.
- Emily must go to school.
- Emily calls the doctor.
- Emily can go to the doctor's at 10.30.

At the doctor's

1. **Before** you listen to the text:
   What do you think the doctor tells Emily?
2. Listen to the text. Find out what the doctor really tells Emily.
   What must she do?

Track 26

No problem. Get well soon! Bye.	– Aaaa –	Is it bad?

No, it isn't bad. You've got the flu. But you mustn't go to school for five days and you must take this medicine.

Hello doctor. I feel really ill.	What's the problem?
OK, now I must take your temperature.	OK, doctor. Thank you.

I've got a sore throat. My head aches and I've got a fever.

I must examine you. Let me see. Open your mouth.	Hello Emily.

3. Look at these text pieces. What does Emily say? What does the doctor say?
   Work with a partner and arrange the text correctly.
4. Write the correct dialogue into your exercise book.
5. Read the dialogue with your partner.

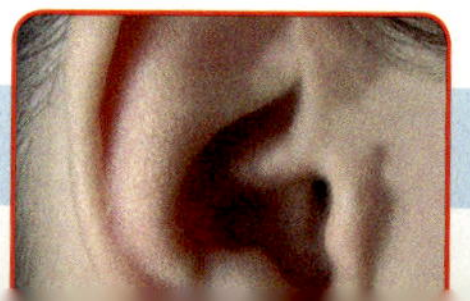

I feel very ill

patient:	doctor:
Good morning, doctor.	Hello (name). What's the problem?
I feel very ill.	
I have got a sore throat. / a broken arm. / a cold. / a headache. / a stomach ache.	
	Just a moment. I must examine you. / take your temperature. / take an X-ray.
Is it bad?	
	No, but you must stay in bed for three days. / take these tablets. / take this medicine.
Thank you, doctor and good bye.	
	Bye bye. Get well soon. / Come back next week.

1. Work with a partner. Write a dialogue together.
   Partner A: You are the patient. You have got a stomach ache.
   Partner B: You tell the patient to stay in bed for two days and to take medicine.
2. Write another dialogue. Act out the scene for your class.

AH

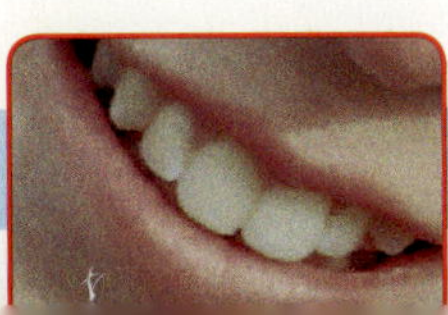

You're lucky!

Track 28

Emily has a sore throat. She can't speak, so she and Paul chat on the internet. Paul is paul94 and Emily is MiMi.

paul94: Hi Emily. Why didn't you come to school today? We wrote an English test.

MiMi: I've got the flu. Oh, my mother mustn't see me now because I really must stay in bed. But I can use the computer.

paul94: Is it bad?

MiMi: No, but I can't speak, I must stay in bed and I must take medicine. It tastes awful.

paul94: Poor Emily! ☹

MiMi: Yes. It's terrible. I mustn't go to school and I can't meet my friends. ☹

paul94: But – hey, you're lucky: You can stay in bed all day! ☺

1. Read the text and find out what Emily should do. Complete the table.

Emily			
can	can't	must	mustn't
use the computer		*stay in bed*	

AH

2. Who is right? Emily or Paul? Is it bad when **you** can't go to school? Discuss in class.

Web page "The flu"

Home

KidsHealth

Track 29

The flu is an infection that causes fever, cough, body aches, headaches, and sometimes earaches.

What can you do? Here are some tips:

- See a doctor. The doctor will tell you if you need to take medicine.
- Drink lots of water and other healthy drinks like orange juice, milk or tea with honey.
- Stay in bed and sleep. If you can't sleep, rest: listen to music, watch a movie on DVD or read a book or magazines.
- Wear warm clothes.
- Wash your hands and use clean paper tissues. Don't give the flu germs to other people.

Most of the time you'll get better in about a week. But if you don't start to feel better, you need to see your doctor again.

http://kidshealth.org/

1. Find out the symptoms of the flu.
2. Add words from this text to your wall frieze.
3. What are the five tips?
   - *You must see a doctor.*
   - *You must drink …*
   - *You must …*
4. Can you think of more tips?

Strategy:

Word clusters

Look at your classroom wall. There are a lot of word cards already. You made them yourselves.
Today we will organise them in a way that they can help you to learn better. This is something that your whole class must do together.

Step 1: Look at the texts from this chapter again. Find all words that come from the word field "doctor".

Step 2: Write the words on cards. Don't write words that are already on the wall.

Step 3: Organise the cards under the following headings:
- At the doctor's
- Illnesses and symptoms
- What the doctor does
- What the patient does

Are there any more headings you can think of?

Step 4: Use sticky tape to put the word cards back on the wall. It should look like this now:

a sore throat
a stomach ache
a headache
a cold
a flu
a broken leg
I must examine you.
You must stay at home.
At the doctor's
You must take the medicine.
You mustn't go to school.
a thermometer
a waiting room
a surgery
an X-ray

Step 5: Put up everything that the class does when working in English – posters, texts, pictures. You will get a wall frieze that shows you what you have learned together.

This is what you have learned

Play in groups of three. You need **one dice**.
One of you is Emily (A), one is her mother (B), one is the doctor (C).

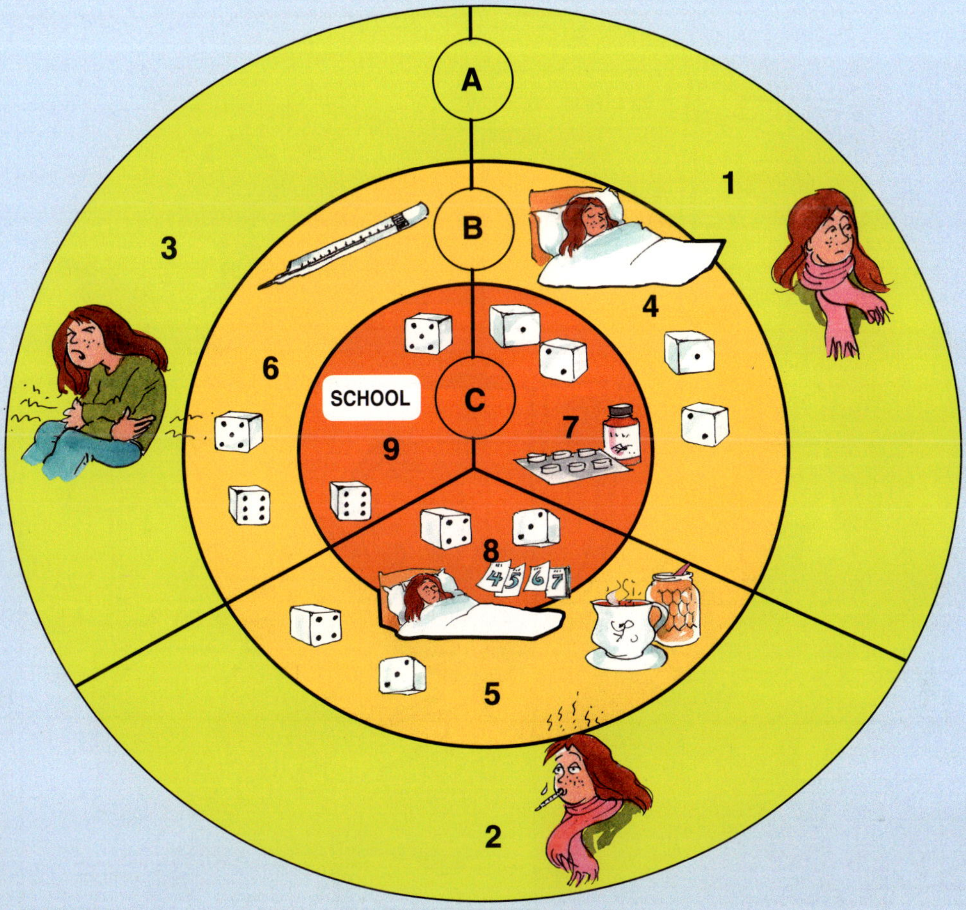

A Roll the dice.
What is the problem?
Say: *I have got …*

B Roll the dice.
What should Emily do?
Say: *You should …*

C Roll the dice.
What must Emily do?
Say: *You must/mustn't …*

Finished? Then change roles and roll the dice again.
Each of you must be Emily at least once.

6 The world of work:

Track 30

Money and jobs

Window-shopping

Track 31

It's Friday afternoon. Emily and Carla go window-shopping in town.

Emily: "Look at these shoes! I like them."
Carla: "They look cool."
Emily: "I really **love** them."
Carla: "They're expensive, Emily."
Emily: "No, I really **want** these shoes."
Carla: "Hello! Emily, wake up! These shoes are very expensive. How much pocket money do you get?"
Emily: "Not enough, that's for sure."
Carla: "How much money do you have in your piggy bank?"
Emily: "I don't know. Let's go home and check."

Emily and Carla walk along. They don't get too far. They stop at the next store.

Carla: "Look, Emily. There's the microphone I talked about."
Emily: "It looks professional."
Carla: "It's perfect."
Emily: "It's expensive, Carla."
Carla: "I know, but I really want it. Let's go home. Today is the day. I will rob my piggy bank."

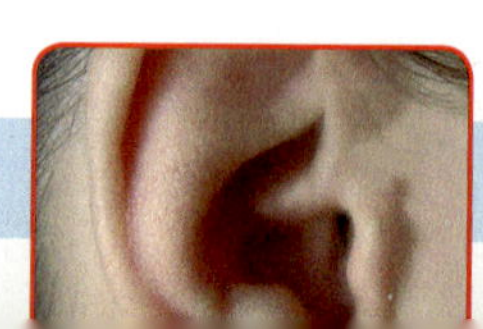

The two girls walk back home. They check their savings.

1. Listen to the text.
2. Read the text.
3. Do you save up money? What for?

AH

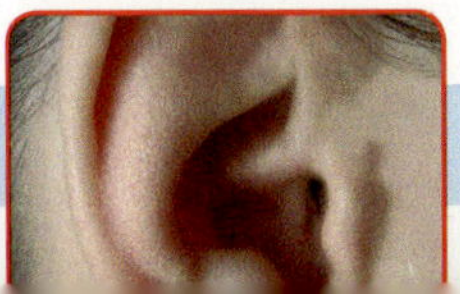

Talking about pocket money

How much pocket money do **you** get?

		50 c	per day.
I	get	€ 5	per week.
		€ 20	per month.

Who gives you the money?

My mother/ my father	gives me	
My parents	give me	the money.
My grand-mother	gives me	

What do you buy with your money?

		cosmetics.
I	buy	sweets.
		DVDs.

AH

1. Talk about pocket money in class.

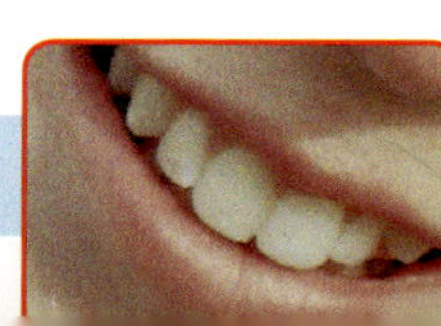

Jobs for teens

You	could	work at a supermarket. baby-sit. clean staircases.

1. What kind of jobs does Carla propose? Make sentences.
2. What else could Emily do? Say:
   She could repair bicycles.

AH

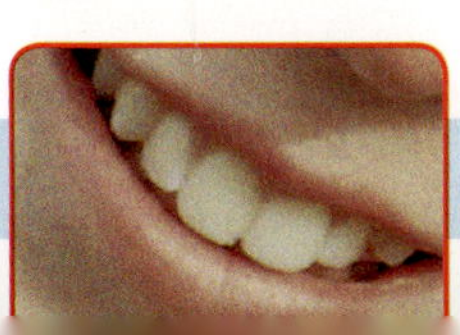

You could, but would you?

I	could	repair bicycles, work at a supermarket, deliver newspapers,	but I wouldn't.

I would baby-sit.

1. What kind of jobs **could** you do, but **would not** do?
2. What kind of jobs **would** you do?

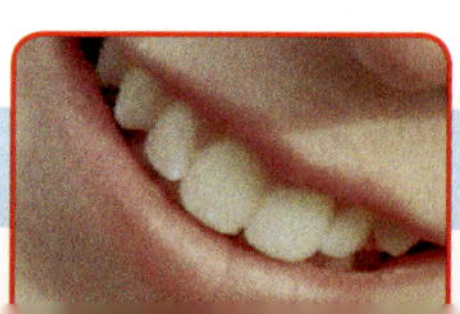

Would you like the job?

	☺	☹
	Yes, because I like cars.	No, because I don't like cleaning.
	Yes, because I'm good at it.	No, because I can't repair bikes.
	Yes, because the job is easy.	No, because I don't like to work outside.
	Yes, because I like to talk to people.	No, because the job is boring.
	Yes, because I like to work outside.	No, because I don't like dirt.

1. Look at the jobs. What is **your** reason? Say the sentences.
2. Find other reasons for or against the jobs.

AH

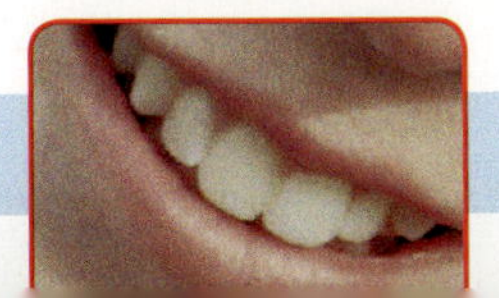

Strategy:

pros and cons

To make up your mind, it often helps to find reasons for (**pros**) or against (**cons**) a certain point. With pros and cons, it's easier to decide what to do next.

Jobs

	pros	cons
to baby-sit	I like children.	I can only work until 8 p.m..
to do gardening	I like to work outside.	It's hard work.
to clean windows	The job is easy.	I hate cleaning.
to walk dogs	I like dogs.	I can't get enough money.

1. Take an A3-sheet of paper.
2. Write down the title at the top.
3. Draw a table like the one above.
4. Find pros and cons.
   Write them down.
5. Look at your reasons. Make a statement.

Planning a flea market

Emily and Carla meet Paul and Cem. They talk about their money problems. They think about what kind of job they could do to earn money.

Track 33

Suddenly Paul has an idea: Let's plan a flea market at our school. Everybody needs money. And a flea market is fun!

What **could** they sell?

1. What could **you** sell?
2. Make a list in class.
3. Plan a flea market in class.

AH

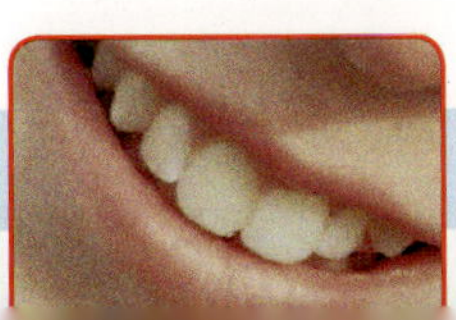

At the flea market

Together with their teacher, Emily, Carla, Paul, Cem and the rest of their class plan a flea market at their school. Some people come to just look at all the things, but many people come to buy something.

AH

1. Read the dialogues.
2. Work with a partner. Think of dialogues and write them down.
3. Act out a flea market scene in class.

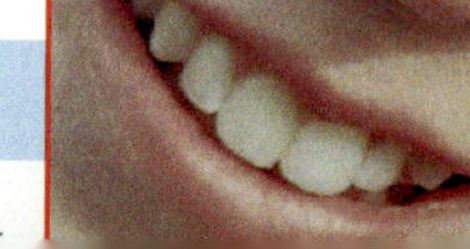

This is what you have learned

Play with a partner. You have 10 minutes.

You need:

- a dice,
- a play piece for each player,
- about 20 chips

Put your piece on start – throw the dice – answer the questions and collect a chip for each correct answer.

Answer in whole sentences. If you land on the same field again, move on to the next field.

The winner is the player with the higher number of chips.

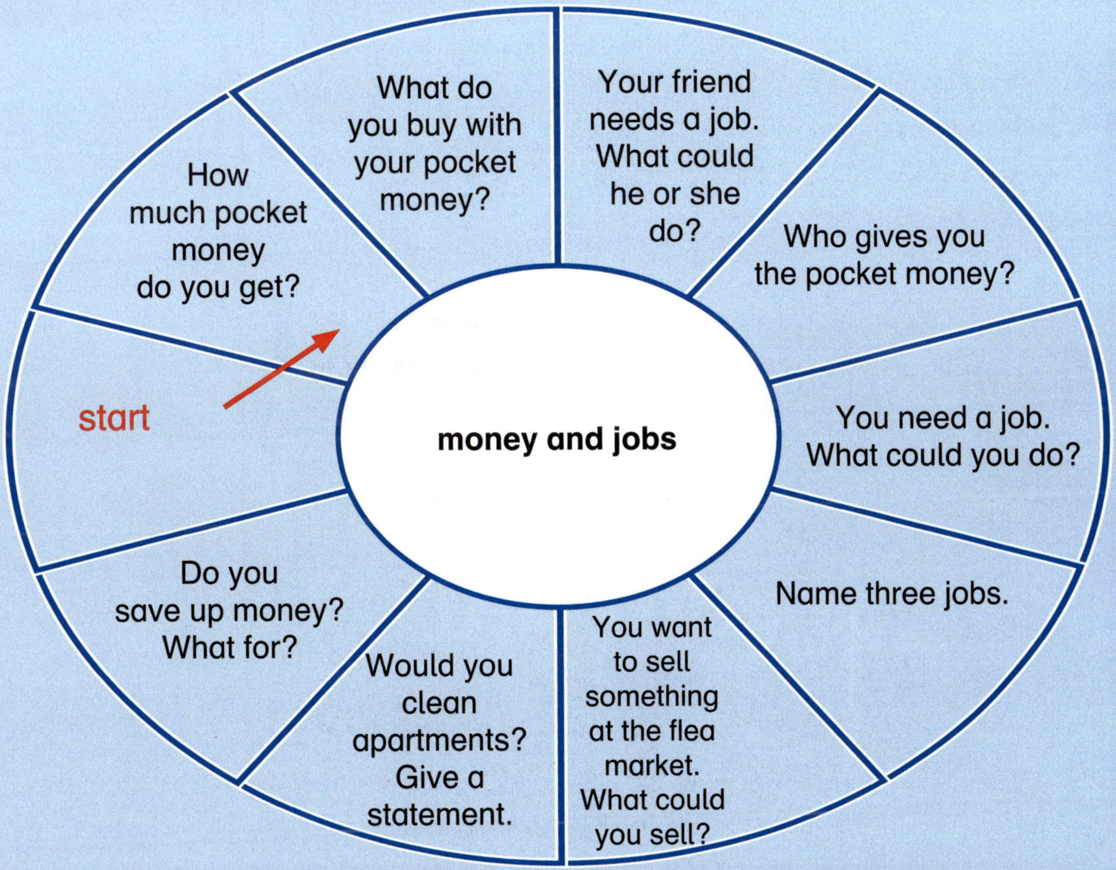

7 Around the house:

Track 35

Energy

Things we use

Track 36 Paul and Emily are in a shop for electrical equipment. The friends want to have a look at different mobile phones.

1. What is important to **you** when you buy a mobile phone? Make a pro and con list.
2. Think about the aspects **design** and **cost**.

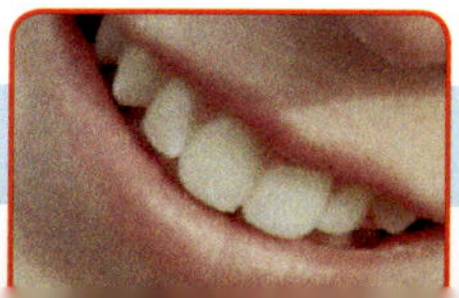

Energy is limited

Paul and Emily are in class. They talk about Emily's new stereo system. The teacher is pleased and impressed that it uses less energy.

Track 37

The teacher asks: "Why did you buy this stereo system?"
"Well, my old one was broken, so I needed a new one. I think it's important to save energy", answers Emily.
"That was very good of you!", says the teacher. "Well done!"

1. What do **you** think? How can **you** save energy? Say:
   I can save energy when …
2. Collect information on the internet and discuss in class.
   When do **you** use energy for example at home or in school?

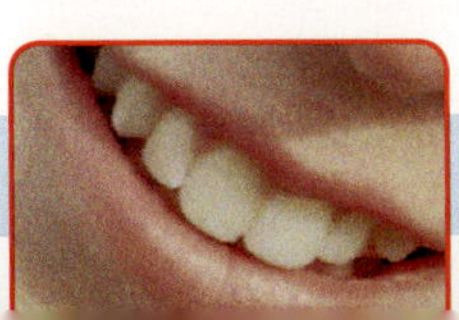

Electricity is everywhere!

1. Which electrical equipment do **you** have at home?
   Collect pictures from magazines.
2. Work in pairs. Divide the pictures into groups. Where can you find the most electrical equipment?
   Use these topics to help you:

- things we have in the living room
- things we have in the kitchen
- things we have in the bathroom
- things we have in the bedroom
- things we have in the hall
- things I have in my room

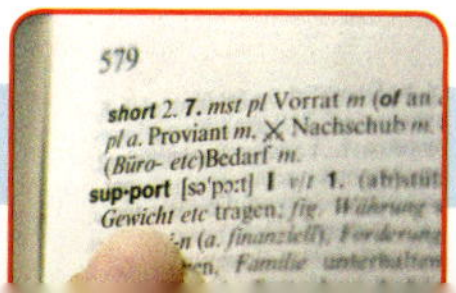

The use of electricity

Energy is everywhere. We all use a lot of energy and natural resources every day. That can be water to wash, oil for cars or electricity, for example.

Track 38

We are so used to electricity that we cannot imagine being without it. Just think: no electric lights, no computer, no television, no fridge to keep food cold, no electric cooker to cook food when you become hungry.

That makes electricity very important for us. But electricity can also be very dangerous.

1. Can you name positive and negative things about electricity? Make a table and complete it.

Electricity is positive because …	Electricity is negative because …
…	…

2. Why is electricity so important for us? Discuss in class.

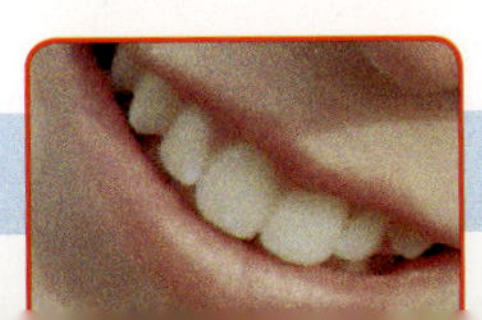

There is a lot of electricity in a house

Track 41

1. What do **you** need to make an electric circuit? Look at the picture. Say: *I need a …*
2. Collect everything that you need and make your own electric circuit. Work in pairs.
3. Why is it called "electric **circuit**"?

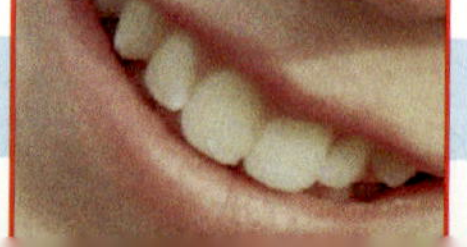

The shoe box house

1. Find an old shoe box.

2. Make furniture from different materials. Choose yourself.

3. Install an electric circuit to light up the house. Gather the following materials: a screwdriver – a battery – a light bulb – a large paperclip (the switch) – three pieces of conducting wire

Strategy:

Mind map

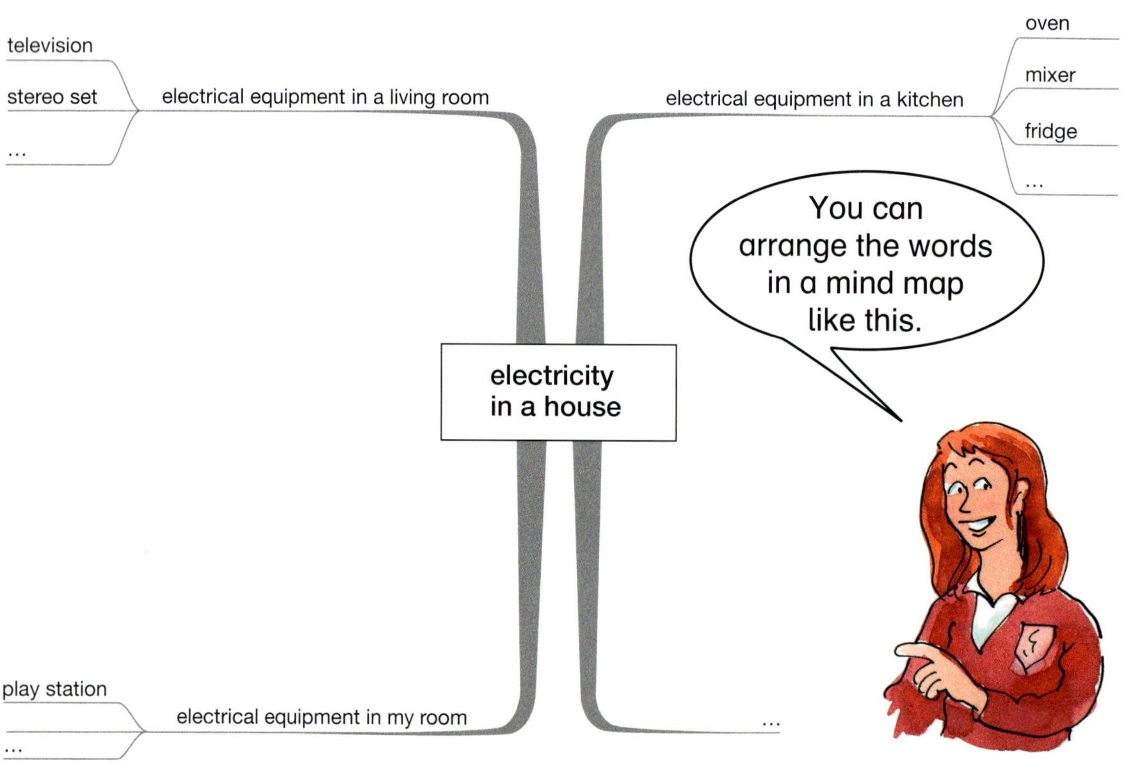

1. Copy the mind map onto an A3-sized sheet of paper.
   Add as many words as you can.
   Work in pairs or groups if you like.

This is what you have learned

In the middle of a garden, in a small toy house, there live two small creatures. One is called Ener, the other is called Gy. Together, Ener and Gy want to light up their house.

Track 42

Gy: "It is very dark in here!"

Ener: "Then why don't you light a candle, Gy?!"

Gy: "Oh, you know you always have to be extra careful with candles. I would really prefer proper electric light."

Ener: "That is a great idea! We will build a really good lighting set!"

Gy: "Great, can we start tomorrow?"

Ener: "No, we can't. We need an electrician, because electricity is as dangerous as candles."

- Name three methods to save energy.
- Name four positive things about electricity.
- Name four negative things about electricity.
- What do you need to make an electric circuit?
- Why is it called "electric circuit"?
- Which electric equipment is in your room?
- Which electric equipment is in your kitchen at home?

8 Around town:

Track 43

a bridge

an information center

a hotel

The class trip

a tower

a street

a city map

a youth hostel

a taxi

a city guide

Where would you like to go?

Track 44

Teacher: "Where would you like to go on a class trip? Please talk about that for a few minutes."

Paul: "Emily, where would you like to go?"
Emily: "Well, I haven't been to London, yet. What do you think?"
Others: "Oh, that is a good idea, Emily."

1. Where would **you** like to go on a class trip? Collect information about the place you would like to visit.
2. Make an information-poster and present it to the class. Work in pairs or small groups.

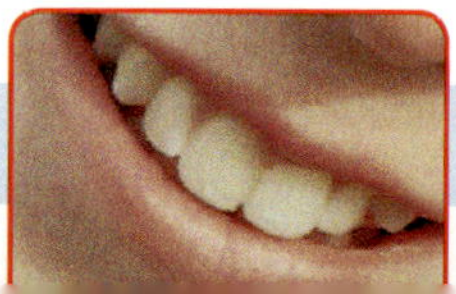

The information-poster

1. Find material to give you information.

2. Cut out information from magazines or from computer prints.

3. Arrange the information on an A3-sized sheet of paper.

Places to visit in London

Track 45

Paul and Emily are on a class trip in London. The friends want to see as many tourist attractions as possible. So they suggest going sight-seeing on a bus.

Paul and Emily are excited, because it´s their first time in London. The rest of the class take loads and loads of photographs.

1. Find famous sights of London. Use books, magazines or the internet to help you. Which London famous sights did you find?
2. Form groups: Choose one famous sight for each group and collect information.
   Present your work to the class.

Things to know about London

Track 46

Paul and Emily are at the Houses of Parliament. They are looking at the building and at Big Ben. It is famous because of its characteristic chime. When it chimes you can hear it almost everywhere in the city of London.

You can buy small replicas of it. It makes a nice souvenir to bring home.

A souvenir is anything you usually buy when you are on holiday. It helps you remember things about your holiday.

1. What is the text about? Collect information in a list.
   Say: *The text is about … .*
2. What is Big Ben?
3. Collect the information and present it to the class.
   Say: *Big Ben is … .*

How to get around London

Track 48

How can we get from Big Ben to Speaker's Corner in Hyde Park?

Well, we could take the tube. I think that's the quickest way.

Paul and Emily look at the tube map. Together with their class they want to visit Speaker's Corner in Hyde Park. To get from Big Ben to Speaker's Corner, they have to take the tube from Westminster to Marble Arch.

Speaker's Corner is famous because you can go there, stand on an old box and talk or argue about anything. You may talk about the bad weather, about your hobbies, politics or opinions.

1. What is the text about? Collect information in a list. You can start like this: *The text is about … .*
2. What is *Speaker's Corner*? Can you find more information?
3. Collect the information and present it to the class. Say: *Speaker's Corner is …*

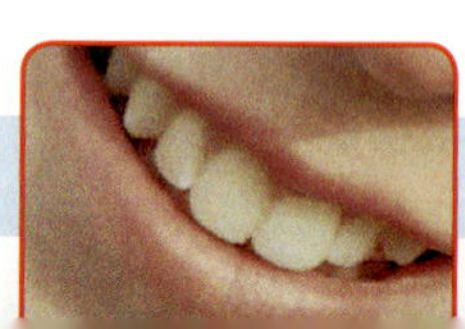

Strategy:

On the tube in London

1. Can you help the class? Find the way from Big Ben at Westminster to Speaker's Corner at Marble Arch. Which underground lines can they go on? Complete:
   To get from Big Ben to Speaker's Corner you must take the ______ line from ______ to ______. Then you must take …
2. Where would you like to go? Use the tube map to find your way. Say:
   To get from …

Key to lines

- Bakerloo
- Central
- Circle
- District
- East London
- Hammersmith & City
- Jubilee
- Metropolitan
- Northern
- Piccadilly
- Victoria
- Waterloo & City
- London Overground

A musical digression: "Streets of London"

Track 50

Streets of London

Have you seen the old man
In the closed-down market
Kicking up the paper,
with his worn out shoes?
In his eyes you see no pride
And held loosely at his side
Yesterday's paper telling yesterday's news

So how can you tell me you're lonely,
And say for you that the sun don't shine?
Let me take you by the hand and lead you through the streets of London
I'll show you something to make you change your mind.

Have you seen the old girl
Who walks the streets of London
Dirt in her hair and her clothes in rags?
She's no time for talking,
She just keeps right on walking
Carrying her home in two carrier bags.

So how can you tell me you're lonely,
And say for you that the sun don't shine?
Let me take you by the hand and lead you through the streets of London
I'll show you something to make you change your mind.

[…]

(Text: Ralph McTell)

1. Listen to the song.
2. Read the lyrics of the song.
3. Can you say what the song is about? Make short notes.

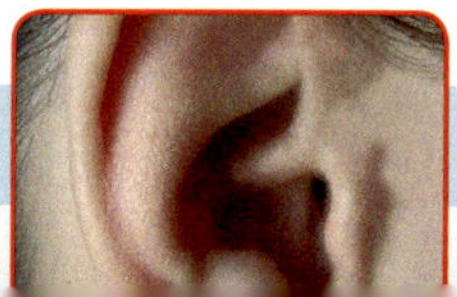

This is what you have learned

Quiz: "About London"

1. Form two teams.
2. Each team rolls a dice.
3. The team with the higher score may answer the first question.
4. Now please close your books.
5. The questions are:
   a Name the capital city of Great Britain.
   b Name a famous building in London.
   c Who or what is "Big Ben"?
   d How many people live in London? Guess!
   e Name three means of public transport in London.
   f What is special about Speaker's Corner in Hyde Park?
   g Who wrote the song "Streets of London"?
6. The team that answers more questions wins the quiz.

Well, how did you do?
Do you know enough about London? ☺

9 Around the world:

Track 51

The news

PEACE in the Middle East!
SPORTS
a microphone
a monitor
a headline

What do daily news consist of?

Track 52

Newsreader on TV: "You will not believe it! England is the new World Champion of Football!"

Dad: "What strange news! When was the last time England won the World Cup?"

Mum: "I don't know. Paul, do you know?"

Paul: "I'm not sure, but I think it was in 1966, wasn't it? They beat Germany in that famous final at Wembley."

Dad: "Let's see what other news there is today."

AH

1. Which topic is the newsreader talking about?
2. What is the scene of Paul and his parents about? Summarise in short sentences.

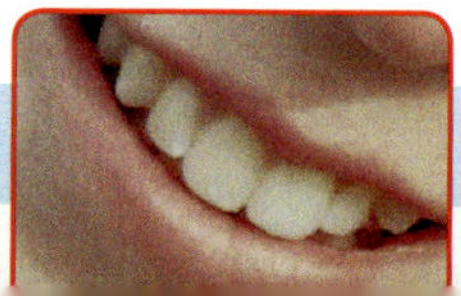

The categories of daily news

1. Which categories are there in daily news?

AH

2. Which tenses do reporters use when they write headlines? Identify the verb in each headline and write it into the correct column. Look at the picture to give you some ideas.

past	present	future
was	is	will be
...	...	...

3. Fill in the missing gaps after you found all the verbs.

Why the news are so important

Track 53

Every day, many things happen in every country all around the world. Some of the things that happen are good; others are not so good. Sometimes the news is very bad. People want to know what's going on in their home town, in their own country or in a different country. That's why they watch the news on TV or why they read a newspaper. The news is important because it informs you about many different topics.

AH

1. About the text: Why do people read or watch the news?
2. Which tense is used in the text? Compare the forms of the verb. Are they in the simple present tense or are they in the simple past?
3. Which tense do Emily and Paul use when they talk about yesterday's news?

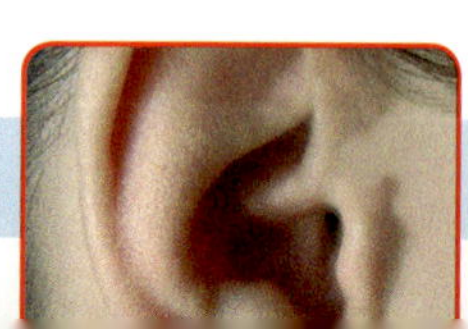

The legend of Finn Mac Cool

Track 55

In Northern Ireland, people tell many legends. One of these legends is that of the Giant's Causeway.
This is the legend:

Many years ago, there was a giant who lived in Northern Ireland. His name was Finn Mac Cool.
One day he met a woman from Scotland. She was also a giant. The two giants fell in love.
They wanted to see each other as often as they could. So to make it easier, Finn started to build a road from Northern Ireland to Scotland. This is what we know today as the Giant's Causeway.
Unfortunately, Finn died before he was able to finish it.

1. What is the text about? Gather information in a list.
   Say: *The text is about … .*
2. What is special about the Giant's Causeway? Can you find information anywhere? Gather the information from the internet and present it to the class.
   Say: *The Giant's Causeway is … .*

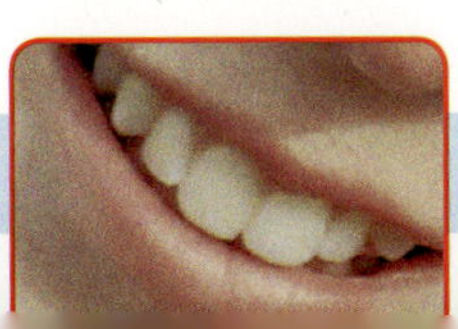

Different themes – different tenses

Here are some headlines to give you ideas.

simple past	simple present	will-future
The Prime Minister **was** in Belfast **yesterday**.	The Prime Minister **is** in Bristol **today**.	The Prime Minister **will be** in London **tomorrow**.
…	…	…

1. Use large sheets of paper in three different colours.
2. Choose one colour for each tense.
3. Cut out headlines from magazines and newspapers and arrange them on the correct paper.
4. Be a reporter: Make your own headlines in different tenses.

Strategy:

Different tenses – different meaning

The Prime Minister **was** in Belfast **yesterday**.

The Prime Minister **is** in Bristol **today**.

The Prime Minister **will be** in London **tomorrow**.

1. Which word changes the meaning of the sentence?
2. Look at all the headlines you gathered earlier. Can you change their meaning? Write down two new ideas like this:

Original: *The weather will be nice and warm tomorrow.*
New 1: *The weather was nice and warm yesterday.*
New 2: *The weather is nice and warm today.*

AH

A musical digression: “A day in the life“

Track 56

A day in the life

I read the news today, oh boy
About a lucky man who made the grade
And though the news was rather sad
Well I just had to laugh
I saw the photograph
He blew his mind out in a car
He didn’t notice that the lights had changed
A crowd of people stood and stared
They’d seen his face before
Nobody was really sure
If he was from the House of Lords.

I saw a film today oh boy
The English Army had just won the war
A crowd of people turned away
but I just had to look
Having read the book
I’d love to turn you on
[…]

(Text: John Lennon/Paul McCartney)

1. Listen to the song.
2. Read the lyrics of the song.
3. Identify the verbs in the lyrics. Which tense did McCartney and Lennon use most?
4. Can **you** say what the song is about? What happens in the song? Make short notes.

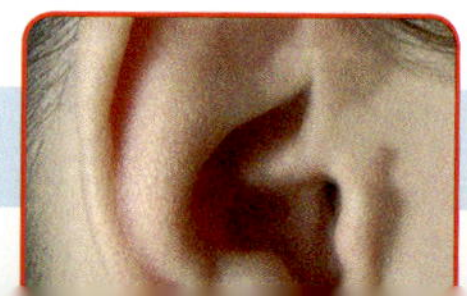

This is what you have learned

Quiz "About tenses"

1. Form two teams.

2. Each team rolls a dice.

3. The team with the higher score may answer the first question.

4. Now please close your books.

5. The questions are:
   a Why are the news important?
   b Name two categories of news.
   c The verb: What does it do?
   d Name the simple past of "to arrive".
   e Name the will-future of "to arrive".
   f Can you remember the rule of how to form the will-future?
   g Can you remember the rule of how to form the simple past?
   h Who wrote the song "A day in the life"?

6. The team that answers more questions wins the quiz.

Well, how did you do?
Do you know enough about tenses? ☺

10 Around the year:

Track 57

Holidays

Martin Luther King
3rd Monday of January
mashed potatoes
a stuffed turkey
4th Thursday of November
a pie
corn
USA
cranberry sauce

Who's your Valentine?

type of hair

Does your Valentine have long hair?

Does your Valentine have curly hair?

colour of hair

Does your Valentine have brown hair?

facial expression

Does your Valentine smile?

Does your Valentine look sad?

colour of the clothes

Does your Valentine wear black clothes?

accessoires

Does your Valentine wear earrings?

Does your Valentine wear a necklace?

1. Work in pairs. Everybody chooses his or her Valentine from the pictures on the next page. Keep it a secret.
2. Ask questions to your partner to find out who her or his Valentine is. Some examples for questions are above.
3. Work out other questions.

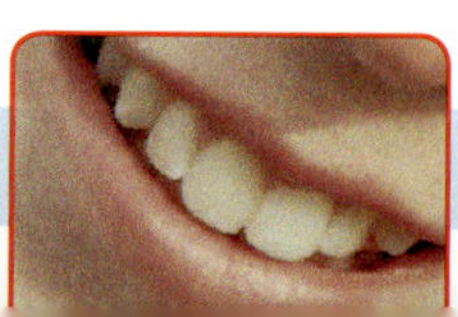

①

②

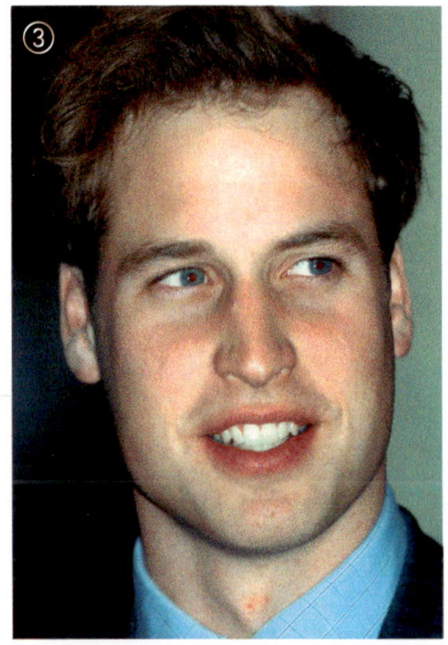
③

④

⑤

⑥

⑦

⑧

⑨

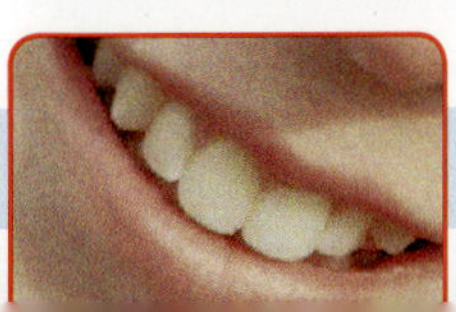

I love you

① Te dua.
② Obicham te.
③ 我愛你
④ Volim te.
⑤ Miluji te.
⑥ Je t´aime.
⑦ lubim ta.
⑧ S`ayapo.
⑨ Ti amo.
⑩ Kimi o ai shiteru.
⑪ Ez te hezdikhem.
⑫ Ya lyublyu tebya.
⑬ Ich liebe Dich.
⑭ Te amo.
⑮ Ik hou van jou.
⑯ Kocham Cie.

1. Above you can see how to say "I love you" in different languages.
   Which languages do you know?

Love is ...

Love is like war:
Easy to begin
but hard
to end.

Love is
a lie.

Love is
the greatest
refresh-
ment.

Love is
you.

Love is
friendship
set on
fire.

AH

2. Write down what you think love is about.
   Love is ...

The first Thanksgiving

Track 58

A long, long time ago, a big ship called "The Mayflower" sailed to America.
It was a long way.
Pilgrims, people who wanted to live in America, were on the ship.
They arrived in winter and so it was very cold.
Because of the long way to America, they had nothing to eat anymore.
The Pilgrims were very hungry. They thought they were alone but suddenly they met other people, Native Americans.
The Native Americans helped the Pilgrims a lot to get along in their new country.
In spring the Native Americans showed the Pilgrims how to plant potatoes, how to plant corn and how to hunt for turkeys. Turkey is a delicious food! The Pilgrims were happy and thankful.
In autumn, after harvest time, the Pilgrims invited the Native Americans for a great dinner.
This was the first **Thanksgiving**.
Nowadays, Thanksgiving is celebrated in the USA on the 4th Thursday of November.

1. Listen and read the text.
2. Look up words you do not know in the dictionary.
3. Is there a similar holiday in Germany?

AH

A Thanksgiving Dinner

Paul's father is American. That's why Paul's family celebrates Thanksgiving.

AH

1. Read the dialogue.
2. Do you like the food in the picture? What do you not like?
3. Have you ever eaten this food?

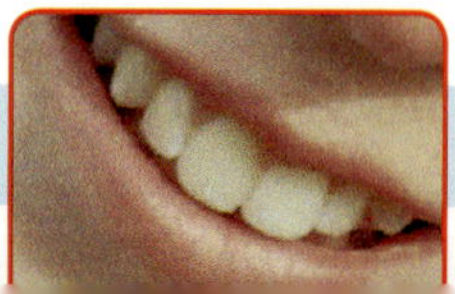

The story of Rosa Parks

Track 59

It was 1st of December, 1955. Rosa Parks was on the way home from work.

Rosa's skin was black, so she had to sit in the back of the bus.

A few bus stops later there were no free seats anymore in the front of the bus.

At the next stop a white man got on the bus.

He looked for a free seat in the front of the bus.

Rosa didn't move further back.

The police arrested Rosa and took her to jail.

Rosa was one of the reasons for the beginning of the fight for equal rights for black and white people.

1. Listen and read the story.
2. Act the story.
3. How did Rosa feel?
4. Have you had a similar experience? How did you feel? Find words to describe for how you felt.

About Martin Luther King Day

Track 60

The birthday of Martin Luther King Jr is on 15th of January, 1929. He grew up in Atlanta, Georgia. Martin Luther King fought against the different treatment of black and white people. White people often had more rights and better conditions than black people. They didn't go to the same schools, restaurants, hotels and parks. In peaceful marches he called for equal treatment (look at the picture below). People now celebrate Martin Luther King's life and dream on the 3rd Monday of January each year. It's been a national holiday since 1986. Martin Luther King was killed on 4th of April, 1968 in Memphis, Tennessee.

1. Read and listen to the text.
2. Look at the picture and read the banners.
3. Look up words which you do not know in the dictionary.

AH

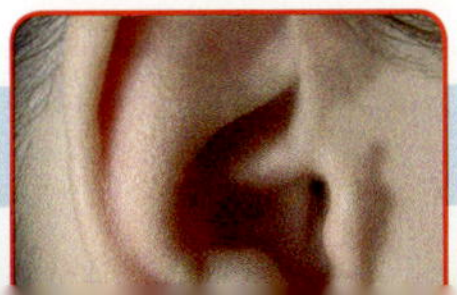

Strategy:

Looking for information

Where and how you can get information

from books and magazines	from the internet	from people
• in libraries	• at home • from friends • at school • in internet cafés	• teachers • experts • contemporary witnesses

Be careful, there is some incorrect information!

1. Look for information about Valentine's Day, Thanksgiving and/or Martin Luther King Day.
2. Present it to the class.
3. Look up words which you do not know in the dictionary.

This is what you have learned

1. Read the sentences.

… is in the USA on the 3rd Monday of January.

… is a national holiday since 1986.

… is similar to the "Erntedankfest" in Germany.

Valentine's Day …

… is to tell lovers and friends how much you love them.

Thanksgiving …

… is named after a man who fought for equal treatment of black and white people.

… was first celebrated by Pilgrims and Native Americans.

Martin Luther King Day …

… is popular for stuffed turkey for dinner.

… is on 14th of February.

2. Draw a table and match the sentences to the correct day.

Valentine's Day	*Thanksgiving*	*Martin Luther King Day*

11 Grammar:

To play with language

To play with language – mit Sprache spielen

Jedes Spiel folgt bestimmten Spielregeln.
Diese Spielregeln musst du kennen und beachten, damit das Spiel funktioniert. Ähnlich ist es mit den Sprachen.
Die englische Sprache folgt bestimmten Regeln der Grammatik.
Wenn du diese Regeln kennst, fällt es dir leichter, eine Sprache zu lernen.
Auf den folgenden Seiten findest du zunächst einige Sprachforscher-Aufgaben (S. 112–116), um mit Sprache zu spielen und die Spielregeln der englischen Sprache kennenzulernen. Im Anschluss folgt eine Zusammenfassung der Sprachregeln (S. 117–129):
die englische Grammatik.

Folgende Tabelle hilft dir, schwierige Wörter besser zu verstehen.

Deutsch	Fachbegriff	Englisch
Hauptwort (Namenwort)	Nomen (Substantiv)	noun
Kurzform		short form
Langform		long form
Einzahl	Singular	singular
Mehrzahl	Plural	plural
Tätigkeitswort (Tuwort, Zeitwort)	Verb	verb
Befehlsform	Imperativ	imperative
Grundform	Infinitiv	infinitive
Hilfsverb, Modalverb		auxiliary verb

Deutsch	Fachbegriff	Englisch
Eigenschaftswort (Wiewort)	Adjektiv	adjective
Verhältniswort	Präposition	preposition
persönliches Fürwort	Personalpronomen	personal pronoun
besitzanzeigendes Fürwort	Possessivpronomen	possessiv pronoun
Gegenwart	Präsens	present tense
einfache Form der Gegenwart	einfaches Präsens	simple present
Vergangenheit	Präteritum	past tense
einfache Form der Vergangenheit	einfaches Präteritum	simple past
Zukunft	Futur	future tense
Zukunft mit „will“		will-future
Verlaufsform der Gegenwart		present progressive
Fragen mit Fragewörtern (Bestimmungsfragen)		questions with question words
Entscheidungsfragen		yes/no questions

Sprachforscher-Aufgaben

1. Mit dem Wort **should** kannst du beschreiben, wie eine Person, ein Gegenstand oder eine Situation sein **sollte**.
   Kannst du folgende Tabelle füllen? Übertrage sie in dein Heft. Ergänze sie mithilfe der Texte im **zweiten Kapitel** (About me).

Was sagst du, wenn du sagen möchtest, ...	Deutsch	Englisch
... dass dein bester Freund dir zuhören sollte?		
... dass deine beste Freundin Musik mögen sollte?		
... dass deine beste Freundin Fußball spielen sollte?		
... dass dein bester Freund nett sein sollte?		
... dass deine beste Freundin Tiere mögen sollte?		
... dass dein bester Freund zu dir halten sollte?		

2. Schaue dir die **should-Sätze** im **zweiten Kapitel** genau an. Welche **Wortart** wird immer direkt **nach** dem Verb (Tätigkeitswort) **should** benutzt? Schreibe die Beispiele so in dein Heft:
   should listen
   should ...

3. Schaue dir die Tabelle auf der Grammatikseite (Seite 117) an. Vergleiche das englische Wort **should** mit dem deutschen Wort **sollte**. Was fällt dir auf? Vergleiche deine Beobachtung mit der deines Nachbarn.

4. In diesem Buch wird häufig die Kurzform und nicht die Langform verwendet. Kurzform heißt, dass die Wörter verkürzt geschrieben werden. Schau dir die Kurzform einmal genauer an, zum Beispiel im **dritten Kapitel** (At school).

   Paul whispers: "I **don't** think hamburger with chips are very healthy."
   The teacher smiles: "**That's** right, Paul."

   Findest du noch mehr Beispiele?

Schreibe die Kurzform auf ein kariertes Papier. Schreibe dabei jeden Buchstaben/jedes Zeichen in einen Karokasten:

d	o	n	’	t

Schreibe darunter die dazugehörige Langform. Statt der Lücke (Leerzeichen) zwischen den Wörtern mache einen dicken Strich zwischen die Karos (kein extra Karo als Leerzeichen!):

d	o	n	o	t

Was fällt dir auf?
Was wurde verkürzt?
Wofür steht das Auslassungszeichen: “ ’ ” ?

5. Wann wird die Kurzform genutzt?
Beantwortet diese Frage mit eurem Partner oder in einer Gruppe.
Jede Gruppe druckt oder kopiert sich eine Seite aus, zum Beispiel aus
– einem englischen Buch (z. B. aus der Bücherei)
– einem englischen Comic (z. B. aus der Bücherei)
– einer englischen Zeitung (z. B. www.guardian.co.uk, www.telegraph.co.uk …)
– einem englischen Interview (mit einem Politiker, mit einem Popstar … aus einer Zeitung/Zeitschrift/Internet)
– einer Gebrauchsanweisung (jede Gebrauchsanweisung hat auch einen englischen Teil …)
– einer englischen Zeitschrift
– einer englischen Homepage
– …
Was fällt euch noch ein?
Vielleicht kennt jemand einen Engländer/Amerikaner/Australier, den er/sie fragen kann?
Unterstreicht Langform und Kurzform in verschiedenen Farben. Was fällt euch auf?
Sammelt eure Ergebnisse und besprecht sie in der Klasse.

6. Im **vierten Kapitel** (Free time) geht es um Pauls Party. Schau dir diese Sätze aus der Geschichte an:

Paul is preparing a fancy dress party.
Emily and Claire are making plans for Paul’s party.
His mum is helping him.
Diese Sätze beschreiben, was jemand jetzt ***gerade*** *macht.*

Schreibe die Sätze in dein Heft. Unterstreiche die zwei Verben (Tätigkeitswörter) in jedem Satz. Was fällt dir auf?
Findest du noch mehr Beispiele?

7. Im **fünften Kapitel** (My body) geht es um einen Arztbesuch. Schau dir die Texte in diesem Kapitel an.

   Wie sagt Emilys Mutter, dass Emily zum Arzt gehen muss?
   Wie sagt die Sprechstundenhilfe, dass Emily vielleicht warten muss?
   Wie sagt der Arzt, dass er bei Emily Fieber messen muss?
   Wie sagt der Arzt, dass er Emily untersuchen muss?
   Wie sagt Emily, dass sie im Bett bleiben muss?
   Wie sagt Emily, dass sie Medizin nehmen muss?

   Schreibe die Sätze untereinander und unterstreiche das Wort für „müssen".

   Suche in den Texten alle Sätze heraus, die das Wort „mustn't" (= must not) enthalten. Findest du eine gute Übersetzung für „mustn't"?

8. Mit dem Wort **could** kannst du beschreiben, was eine Person tun **könnte** oder wie eine Person, ein Gegenstand oder eine Situation sein könnte.

   Mit dem Wort **would**, kannst du beschreiben, was eine Person tun **würde** oder wie eine Person oder ein Gegenstand sein **würde**.

   Schaue dir folgende Sätze an. Was fällt dir an den Modalverben **could** und **would** auf?

   *You **could** clean windows.*
   *She **could** repair bicycles.*
   *We **could** wash cars.*

   *I **would** plan a flea market.*
   *He **would** walk dogs.*
   *They **would** deliver newspapers.*

9. Vergleiche die Modalverben **could** und **would** mit dem Modalverb **should** aus Kapitel 2 (About me). Vergleiche deine Beobachtungen mit deinem Nachbarn.

10. Schaue dir das **sechste Kapitel** (The world of work) genau an. Schreibe fünf Sätze mit Übersetzung so in dein Heft:

I could baby-sit but I wouldn't baby-sit.	Ich könnte babysitten, aber ich würde nicht babysitten.

11. Im **siebten Kapitel** (Around the house) sollst du einen Schuhkarton beleuchten. Schaue dir die Arbeitsaufträge im Arbeitsheft an. Schreibe jeweils das erste Wort jedes Satzes in dein Heft – die Befehlsform. Vergleiche die Formen. Wie wird die Befehlsform gebildet? Hilfe findest du im Grammatikteil auf Seite 124.

12. Wenn du sagen möchtest, dass ein Ereignis in der Vergangenheit, der Gegenwart oder in der Zukunft liegt, musst du die Form eines bestimmten Wortes verändern.

Welches Wort ist für die Zeitform verantwortlich?
Hier zeigen wir dir ein Beispiel:

simple past (Vergangenheit)	simple present (Gegenwart)	will-future (Zukunft)
The Prime Minister **arrived** in Belfast, **yesterday**.	The Prime Minister **arrives** in Bristol, **today**.	The Prime Minister **will arrive** in London, **tomorrow**.

Was ist in den drei Sätzen in der Tabelle gleich?
Was ist unterschiedlich?
Versuche die Unterschiede zu benennen.
Hilfe findest du im Grammatikteil auf Seite 125.

13. Im **zehnten Kapitel** (Around the year) werden Fragen mit „to do" gebildet. Schreibe folgende Sätze in dein Heft.

Do Paul and Emily wear glasses?
Do Claire and Rob have blond hair?
Do you wear blue clothes?
Does Emily wear earrings?
Does Rob have long hair?
Does Claire wear a necklace?

Unterstreiche in jedem Satz das „do" bzw. „does".

Was fällt Dir auf?

Wann wird „do" und wann wird „does" verwendet?

14. Schreibe folgende Sätze wie dargestellt untereinander in dein Heft.

	Rob	has	long hair.
① Does	Rob	have	long hair?
	Emily	wears	a necklace.
② Does	Emily	wear	a necklace?
	It	rains.	
③ Does	it	rain?	

Unterstreiche die Veränderung bei den Fragesätzen.

Zusammenfassung der Sprachregeln

Kapitel 2: Das Modalverb should

Wenn du ausdrücken möchtest, wie eine Person, ein Gegenstand oder eine Situation sein **sollte**, benutzt du das sogenannte Modalverb **should**.

Englisch	Deutsch
I should	ich sollte
you should	du solltest/Sie (Siezform) sollten
he should	er sollte
she should	sie sollte
it should	es sollte
we should	wir sollten
you should	ihr solltet/Sie (Siezform) sollten
they should	sie sollten

He should help me. (Er sollte mir helfen.)

She should like music. (Sie sollte Musik mögen.)

I should go to the doctor. (Ich sollte zum Arzt gehen.)

We should talk to each other. (Wir sollten miteinander reden.)

Kapitel 3: Lang- und Kurzform

It is a wonderful day today.

I have got a dog. He is nice.

I do not know …

I am hungry!

It's a wonderful day today.

I've got a dog. He is nice.

I don't know …

I'm hungry!

Langform (Long form)

Kurzform (Short form)

In der Langform werden alle Wörter ausgeschrieben (z. B.: I **am** hungry).
In der Kurzform werden manche Wörter verkürzt geschrieben (z. B.: I**'m** hungry). Das heißt, dass Buchstaben weggelassen werden (statt **I am** nur **I'm**).
Das Zeichen „ **'** “ bei **I'm** zeigt, dass hier etwas weggelassen wurde.
Die Kurzform kann nicht alleine stehen, sondern hängt sich immer an das Wort davor an (nicht: ~~I 'm~~ sondern: **I'm**).

Beide Formen werden im Englischen genutzt. Beim Sprechen verwendest du meist die Kurzform, beim Schreiben die Langform. Wird ein Gespräch aufgeschrieben, wird meist die Kurzform verwendet. Deswegen musst du beide verstehen und benutzen können.

Langform	Kurzform
not	n't
I do not eat cheese.	I don't eat cheese.
She does not like it.	She doesn't like it.
I cannot do that.	I can't do that.
(!) nicht: ~~can not~~!	(!) nicht: ~~cann't~~

not	n't
I could not come.	I couldn't come.
I would not lie.	I wouldn't lie.

am	'm
I am Emily.	I'm Emily.

is	's
He is nice.	He's nice.

are	're
We are hungry.	We're hungry.
You are right.	You're right.
(!) ***your = dein, aber: you're = du bist/ihr seid***	

will	'll
I will find you.	I'll find you.

have	've
You have got a friend.	You've got a friend.

Kapitel 4: Die Verlaufsform der Gegenwart *(present progressive)*

Wenn du sagen möchtest, dass jemand etwas **jetzt gerade** macht, benutzt du die Verlaufsform. Die Verlaufsform drückt einen Vorgang aus, der noch nicht zu Ende ist.

So bildest du die Verlaufsform:

Merke  + am/is/are/'m/'s/'re + Grundform des Tätigkeitsworts mit ing

Englisch	**Deutsch**
I am playing. (I'm playing.)	Ich spiele jetzt gerade.
You are playing. (You're playing.)	Du spielst jetzt gerade.
He is playing. (He's playing.)	Er spielt jetzt gerade.
She is playing. (She's playing.)	Sie spielt jetzt gerade.
It is playing. (It's playing.)	Es spielt jetzt gerade.
We are playing. (We're playing.)	Wir spielen jetzt gerade.
You are playing. (You're playing.)	Ihr spielt jetzt gerade.
They are playing. (They're playing.)	Sie spielen jetzt gerade.

Wenn das Verb (Tätigkeitswort) mit einem **„e“** aufhört, lässt man das **„e“** bei der ing-Form weg: to prepare → preparing

to swim → swimming

Verneinung der Verlaufsform

Wenn du sagen möchtest, dass jemand etwas jetzt gerade **nicht** macht, stellst du **not** vor das Tätigkeitswort mit ing:

You are **not** playing.
Kurzform:
You aren**'t** playing. (Du spielst jetzt gerade nicht.)
I'm **not** playing. (Ich spiele jetzt gerade nicht.)

Merke  + am/is/are/'m/'s/'re + **not** + Grundform des Tätigkeitsworts mit ing

Entscheidungsfragen

Wenn du wissen möchtest, ob jemand etwas gerade tut, fragst du:

Are you playing? (Spielst du jetzt gerade?)
Is she playing? (Spielt sie jetzt gerade?)

Merke Am/Is/Are +  + Grundform des Tätigkeitsworts mit ing + ?

Kapitel 5: Das Modalverb „must/mustn't"

Must und *mustn't* sind Modalverben. Nach Modalverben steht immer ein Verb (Tätigkeitswort) in der Grundform. Die Form ist bei allen Fürwörtern gleich.

I must examine you.
He must examine you.
We must examine you.

Vorsicht bei *„mustn't"*:
Mustn't heißt nämlich „etwas nicht dürfen".

I **mustn't** go to school (Ich **darf nicht** in die Schule **gehen**.)

Übrigens: *Have to/has to* haben die gleiche Bedeutung wie must. Immer wenn du im Englischen das Wort *„must"* benutzt, kannst du statt dessen auch *„have to"* oder *„has to"* benutzen.

I must examine you. = **I have** to examine you.
He must examine you. = **He has** to examine you.

Das ist vor allem wichtig, wenn:

du sagen willst, dass jemand etwas nicht tun muss:
I **don't have to** examine you.

du sagen willst, dass jemand etwas tun musste:
He **had to** examine me.

Kapitel 6: Die Modalverben could und would

Wenn du ausdrücken möchtest, wie eine Person, ein Gegenstand oder eine Situation sein **könnte**, benutzt du das sogenannte Modalverb **could**.

Wenn du ausdrücken möchtest, was du tun **würdest** oder wie eine Person oder ein Gegenstand sein **würde**, benutzt du das Modalverb **would**.

could		would	
Englisch	Deutsch	Englisch	Deutsch
I could	ich könnte	I would	ich würde
you could	du könntest/ Sie (Siezform) könnten	you would	du würdest/ Sie (Siezform) würden
he could	er könnte	he would	er würde
she could	sie könnte	she would	sie würde
it could	es könnte	it would	es würde
we could	wir könnten	we would	wir würden
you could	ihr könntet/ Sie (Siezform) könnten	you would	ihr würdet/ Sie (Siezform) würden
they could	sie könnten	they would	sie würden

I could wash cars. (Ich könnte Autos waschen.)
He could baby-sit. (Er könnte babysitten.)
We could clean windows. (Wir könnten Fenster putzen.)

You would walk dogs. (Du würdest Hunde ausführen.)
She would deliver newspapers. (Sie würde Zeitungen austragen.)
They would sell things. (Sie würden Dinge verkaufen.)

Kapitel 7: Die Befehlsform

Wenn du einer oder mehreren Person/-en etwas befehlen möchtest oder sie auffordern möchtest, etwas zu tun, benutzt du die Befehlsform. Sie lautet wie die Grundform des Verbs.

Zum Beispiel findet sich die Befehlsform in Arbeitsanweisungen:
(to find) => **Find** an old shoe box. (Finde einen alten Schuhkarton.)
(to make) => **Make** furniture from different materials. (Stelle Möbel aus unterschiedlichen Materialien her.)
(to install) => **Install** an electric circuit to light the house up. (Beleuchte das Haus durch einen Stromkreis.)

Die verneinte Befehlsform wird in Einzahl und Mehrzahl mit „don't + Grundform eines Verbs“ gebildet.
Don't play in the bathroom. (Spiele nicht im Badezimmer.)

Kapitel 8: Das Modalverb can

Wenn du sagen möchtest, dass jemand etwas kann oder nicht kann, benutzt du das Verb **can**.
Es wird in Verbindung mit der Grundform eines Verbs benutzt.

Zum Beispiel:
He **can play** billards. (Er kann Billard spielen.)

Die verneinte Form heißt **cannot** (Kurzform: can't).
He cannot play billards. (Er kann kein Billard spielen.)

Das Verb **can** lautet in allen Personen gleich.
So how **can** you **tell** me you're lonely?
(Wie kannst du mir sagen, dass du einsam bist?)
So how **can** she **tell** me you're lonely?
(Wie kann sie mir sagen, dass du einsam bist?)
So how **can** they **tell** me you're lonely?
(Wie können sie mir sagen, dass du einsam bist?)

Kapitel 9: Das Verb in drei Zeitformen

Wenn du ausdrücken möchtest, dass ein Ereignis in einer anderen Zeit als in der Gegenwart liegt, dann musst du die Form des Verbs (Tätigkeitswortes) verändern.
Hier verdeutlichen wir das einmal am Beispiel
„to arrive – ankommen“ und vergleichen die einfache Form der Gegenwart (simple present) mit der einfachen Form der Vergangenheit (simple past).

Gegenwart *(simple present)*					
Englisch			Deutsch		
I	arrive	today.	Ich	komme	heute an.
You	arrive	today.	Du	kommst	heute an.
He	arrives	today.	Er	kommt	heute an.
She	arrives	today.	Sie	kommt	heute an.
It	arrives	today.	Es	kommt	heute an.
We	arrive	today.	Wir	kommen	heute an.
You	arrive	today.	Ihr	kommt	heute an.
They	arrive	today.	Sie	kommen	heute an.

Vergangenheit *(simple past)*					
Englisch			Deutsch		
I	arrived	yesterday.	Ich	kam	gestern an.
You	arrived	yesterday.	Du	kamst	gestern an.
He	arrived	yesterday.	Er	kam	gestern an.
She	arrived	yesterday.	Sie	kam	gestern an.
It	arrived	yesterday.	Es	kam	gestern an.
We	arrived	yesterday.	Wir	kamen	gestern an.
You	arrived	yesterday.	Ihr	kamt	gestern an.
They	arrived	yesterday.	Sie	kamen	gestern an.

11 Grammar:

Um aus dem simple present das simple past zu formen, muss die Endung des Verbs verändert werden.

Merke

⇒ I arrive today. — Ich komme heute an.

Grundform des Verbs
+ **ed**

⇒ I arri**ved** yesterday. — Ich kam gestern an.

Diese Regel gilt für alle **regelmäßigen** Tätigkeitswörter.
Aber es gibt auch **unregelmäßige** Tätigkeitswörter.

„to be – sein" ist dafür ein Beispiel:

simple present					
Englisch			Deutsch		
I	am	at school today.	Ich	bin	heute in der Schule.
You	are	at school today.	Du	bist	heute in der Schule.
He	is	at school today.	Er	ist	heute in der Schule.
She	is	at school today.	Sie	ist	heute in der Schule.
It	is	at school today.	Es	ist	heute in der Schule.
We	are	at school today.	Wir	sind	heute in der Schule.
You	are	at school today.	Ihr	seid	heute in der Schule.
They	are	at school today.	Sie	sind	heute in der Schule.

Eine Liste weiterer unregelmäßige Tätigkeitswörter findest du auf Seite 130.

Die Formen des simple past bei **„to be – sein“** kannst du dir ganz einfach merken:

simple past					
Englisch			Deutsch		
I	was	at school yesterday.	Ich	war	gestern in der Schule.
You	were	at school yesterday.	Du	warst	gestern in der Schule.
He	was	at school yesterday.	Er	war	gestern in der Schule.
She	was	at school yesterday.	Sie	war	gestern in der Schule.
It	was	at school yesterday.	Es	war	gestern in der Schule.
We	were	at school yesterday.	Wir	waren	gestern in der Schule.
You	were	at school yesterday.	Ihr	wart	gestern in der Schule.
They	were	at school yesterday.	Sie	waren	gestern in der Schule.

11 Grammar:

Wenn du ausdrücken möchtest, dass ein Ereignis in der Zukunft (future) liegen wird, dann musst du die Form des Verbs verändern.

will-future					
Englisch			Deutsch		
I	will be	at school tomorrow.	Ich	werde	morgen in der Schule sein.
You	will be	at school tomorrow.	Du	wirst	morgen in der Schule sein.
He	will be	at school tomorrow.	Er	wird	morgen in der Schule sein.
She	will be	at school tomorrow.	Sie	wird	morgen in der Schule sein.
It	will be	at school tomorrow.	Es	wird	morgen in der Schule sein.
We	will be	at school tomorrow.	Wir	werden	morgen in der Schule sein.
You	will be	at school tomorrow.	Ihr	werdet	morgen in der Schule sein.
They	will be	at school tomorrow.	Sie	werden	morgen in der Schule sein.

Es ist ganz einfach, das will-future zu bilden:

Merke  + will + Grundform des Verbs + Rest des Satzes.

Kapitel 10: Fragen mit „to do“

Wie man Fragen mit Fragewörtern bildet, hast du bereits gelernt (Schülerbuch 5/6, S. 123).
Wie kann man Fragen ohne Fragewörter stellen?
Dazu benötigst du *„do“* bzw. *„does“*.

1. Satz in der Gegenwart:
   Paul and Emily wear glasses. (Paul und Emily tragen eine Brille.)
2. Setze „do“ an den Satzanfang und stelle die Frage:
   Do Emily and Paul wear glasses? (Tragen Paul und Emily eine Brille?)

	Paul and Emily	wear	glasses.
Do	Paul and Emily	wear	glasses?

Bei he/she/it musst du *does* verwenden!
Zusätzlich muss das Verb in die Grundform verwandelt werden!

1. Satz in der Gegenwart:
   Paul wears glasses. (Paul trägt eine Brille.)
2. Setze *does* an den Satzanfang und verwende die Grundform des Verbs.
   Does Paul wear glasses? (Trägt Paul eine Brille?)

	Paul	wears	glasses.
Does	Paul	wear	glasses?

Das **„does“** übernimmt das „s“ vom Verb.

Unregelmäßige Verben

Grundform	Vergangenheit	Deutsch
to be	was/were	sein, war
to beat	beat	schlagen, schlug
to begin	began	beginnen, begann
to blow	blew	blasen, blies
to break	broke	brechen, brach
to bring	brought	bringen, brachte
to buy	bought	kaufen, kaufte
to choose	chose	auswählen, aussuchen, wählte aus
to come	came	kommen, kam
to do	did	tun, tat
to draw	drew	zeichnen, zeichnete
to drink	drank	trinken, trank
to eat	ate	essen, aß
to fall	fell	fallen, fiel
to feel	felt	fühlen, fühlte
to forget	forgot	vergessen, vergaß
to get	got	bekommen, gelangen, bekam
to give	gave	geben, gab
to grow up	grew up	aufwachsen, wuchs auf
to have	had	haben, hatte
to keep	kept	halten, hielt

Grundform	Vergangenheit	Deutsch
to know	knew	wissen, wusste
to leave	left	verlassen, verließ
to make	made	machen, machte
to meet	met	treffen, traf
to read	read	lesen, las
to see	saw	sehen, sah
to sing	sang	singen, sang
to sleep	slept	schlafen, schlief
to speak	spoke	sprechen, sprach
to stand up	stood up	aufstehen, stand auf
to swim	swam	schwimmen, schwamm
to take	took	nehmen, nahm
to teach	taught	unterrichten, beibringen, unterrichtete
to tell	told	mitteilen, erzählen, sagen, sagte
to think	thought	denken, dachte
to throw	threw	werfen, warf
to wear	wore	tragen, trug
to write	wrote	schreiben, schrieb

A

	a	– ein, eine
	A4-sized	– A4-formatig
	about	– über, ungefähr
	above	– oben
an	accessory, (pl. accessories)	– ein Accessoire, (Accessoires)
to	ache	– weh tun, schmerzen
to	act	– schauspielern
to	act out	– durchspielen
an	activity	– eine Aktivität
to	add	– hinzufügen
an	adjective	– ein Adjektiv
	after	– nach
	again	– noch einmal, wieder
	against	– gegen
	ago	– vor, vergangen
	almost	– fast
	alone	– allein
	alphabetically	– alphabetisch
	already	– schon, bereits
	alright	– in Ordnung
	also	– auch
	aluminium foil	– Alufolie
	always	– immer
	and	– und
	another	– ein anderer/eine andere/ein anderes
to	answer	– antworten
	anymore	– mehr
an	apartment	– eine Wohnung
	apple juice	– Apfelsaft
	applesauce	– Apfelmus
	April	– April
	are	– sind
an	argument	– ein Argument
to	arrange	– arrangieren, planen
to	arrest	– festnehmen
to	arrive	– ankommen
	arrogant	– arrogant
	as	– wie (im Vergleich)
to	ask	– fragen, bitten
	at	– am, an
	at school	– in der Schule
	attraction	– Attraktion
	August	– August
	autumn	– Herbst
	awful	– schrecklich, furchtbar

B

to	baby-sit	– babysitten
	back	– zurück, hinten
	backward	– rückwärts
	bacon	– Speck
	bad	– schlecht, schlimm
to	bake	– backen
a	baked potato	– eine Ofenkartoffel
a	band	– eine Musikgruppe
a	banner	– ein Transparent
a	basketball	– ein Basketball
a	battery	– eine Batterie
to	be	– sein
to	be called	– genannt werden
to	be careful	– vorsichtig sein, achtsam sein
to	be clean	– sauber sein
to	be dead	– tot sein
to	be down	– traurig, deprimiert sein
to	be excited	– aufgeregt sein
to	be fun	– spaßig, lustig sein

to	be fun-orientated	– spaßorientiert sein
to	be in love	– verliebt sein
to	be sorry about something	– leid tun wegen einer Sache
to	be sure	– sicher sein
to	be thankful	– dankbar sein
to	be tired of something	– auf etwas keine Lust mehr haben
to	be white	– weiß sein
to	be with someone	– bei jemandem sein
	beans	– Bohnen
to	beat	– schlagen
	beautiful	– schön
	because	– weil
	because of	– wegen, aufgrund
a	bed	– ein Bett
	before	– bevor, vorher, vor (zeitlich)
to	begin	– anfangen
a	beginning	– ein Anfang
	Belfast	– Hauptstadt von Nordirland
to	believe	– glauben
	below	– unten
a	bench	– eine Bank
to	bend	– beugen
	best	– beste, bester
	better	– besser
	between	– zwischen
a	bicycle/bike	– ein Fahrrad, ein Rad
	big	– groß
	bigger	– größer
the	biggest	– der, die, das größte
	billiards	– das Billardspiel
a	birthday	– ein Geburtstag
to	be black	– schwarz sein
	black	– schwarz
	black people	– Schwarze
to	blow	– blasen
a	boat trip	– eine Bootsfahrt
a	book	– ein Buch
	boring	– langweilig
a	bottle	– eine Flasche
a	bowl	– eine Schüssel
a	boyfriend	– ein Freund (Liebesbeziehung)
	bread	– ein Brot
to	break	– brechen
a	bridge	– eine Brücke
	bright	– grell
to	bring	– bringen
	broken	– gebrochen, zerbrochen (Vergangenheitsform von „to break“)
a	broken leg	– ein gebrochenes Bein
a	brother	– ein Bruder
	brown	– braun
to	build	– bauen
a	building	– ein Gebäude
a	bulb	– eine Glühbirne
a	bun	– ein Brötchen
a	bus	– ein Bus
a	bus stop	– eine Bushaltestelle
	busy	– beschäftigt sein
	but	– aber
	butter	– Butter
a	butterfly	– ein Schmetterling
to	buy	– kaufen

C

a	cafeteria	– eine Kantine
to	call	– jemanden anrufen

a	camera	– ein Fotoapparat
	can	– können
a	candle	– eine Kerze; eine Glühlampe
a	cap	– ein Käppi
a	car	– ein Auto
a	card	– eine Karte
to	care about someone	– sich um jemanden kümmern oder sorgen; den anderen wertschätzen
	careful	– vorsichtig
a	carrot	– eine Karotte
a	cartoon	– ein Zeichentrickfilm
a	category(pl. categories)	– eine Kategorie (Kategorien)
to	cause	– verursachen
to	celebrate	– feiern
a	central heating	– eine Zentralheizung
	certain	– bestimmte, bestimmtes, bestimmter
a	champion	– ein Meister
to	change	– ändern, wechseln
to	change	– verändern
a	change	– eine Veränderung
a	character	– ein Charakter
	characteristic	– charakteristisch
to	chat	– sich im Netz unterhalten
	cheap	– billig
to	check	– überprüfen
	cheddar cheese	– Cheddar Käse (rötlicher Käse)
	cheese	– Käse
a	cheese	– ein Käse
a	chicken	– ein Huhn
a	child (pl. children)	– ein Kind (pl. Kinder)
a	chime	– ein Glockenschlag
a	chip	– eine Spielmünze
a	chocolate	– eine Schokolade
	chocolate	– Schokolade
a	chocolate pudding	– ein Schokoladenpudding
to	choose	– auswählen, aussuchen
	Christmas Eve	– Heiligabend
a	chunk	– ein Stück
to	circle	– umkreisen
a	circuit	– ein (Strom-)Kreis
a	city guide	– ein Stadtführer
a	city map	– eine Stadtkarte, ein Stadtplan
a	claim	– eine Forderung
to	clap	– klatschen
a	class	– eine Klasse
a	class trip	– eine Klassenfahrt
a	classmate	– ein Klassenkamerad
to	clean	– sauber machen
	clean	– sauber
to	clear	– klären, säubern
a	cloak	– ein Umhang
	close	– nahe
	clothes	– Kleidung
a	cocktail	– ein Cocktail
a	cold	– eine Erkältung, Schnupfen
	cold	– kalt
to	collect	– sammeln
a	collection	– eine Sammlung
a	colour	– eine Farbe
to	colour	– (an)malen
to	come	– kommen
a	comic	– ein Comicheft

to	compare	– vergleichen
a	comparison	– ein Vergleich
a	computer	– ein Computer
a	computer game	– ein Computerspiel
a	condition	– Bedingung, Voraussetzung
a	conducting wire	– ein Leitungsdraht
	congratulations	– Glückwünsche
to	consist of	– aus … bestehen
a	contemporary witness	– ein Zeitzeuge
	contra	– gegen
a	cooker	– ein Herd
a	cookie	– ein Keks
	cool	– cool, kühl
	corn	– Mais
	correct	– korrekt
	cosmetics	– Kosmetik
	could	– könnte
a	country	– ein Land
to	cover something	– etwas bedecken
	crackers	– Kekse (salzige)
	cranberry sauce	– Preiselbeersauce
	creative	– kreativ
a	creature	– eine Kreatur, ein Wesen
to	cross off	– durchstreichen
to	cross something out	– etwas durchstreichen
a	crowd	– eine Menschenmenge
to	cry	– weinen
a	cucumber	– eine Gurke
	curly	– lockig
to	cut	– schneiden
a	cut	– ein Schnitt
to	cut	– schneiden

D

a	dad	– ein Papa, ein Vater
	daily	– täglich
to	dance	– tanzen
a	dance	– ein Tanz
	dangerous	– gefährlich
	dark	– dunkel
a	day	– ein Tag
	dear	– Liebes
	death	– der Tod
	December	– Dezember
to	decide	– entscheiden
to	decorate	– schmücken
	decorations	– Dekorationen
	deep	– tief
	delicious	– köstlich
to	deliver	– austeilen, vorbei bringen
to	demonstrate	– demonstrieren, protestieren
to	describe	– beschreiben
to	design	– gestalten
a	dialogue	– ein Dialog
a	dice	– ein Würfel
a	dictionary	– ein Wörterbuch
to	die	– sterben
a	difference	– ein Unterschied
	different	– unterschiedlich, verschieden, anders
	dinner	– Abendessen
a	direction	– eine Richtung
	dirty	– schmutzig
to	discuss	– diskutieren
to	do	– tun
a	doctor	– ein Arzt
a	dog	– ein Hund
	don't = do not	– nicht tun
	downtown	– die Innenstadt
to	draw	– zeichnen

a	dream	– ein Traum
to	drink	– trinken
	during	– während

E

	each	– jeder, jede, jedes
	each other	– einander
to	earn	– verdienen
	earrings	– Ohrringe
	easy	– einfach
	easier	– einfacher
to	eat	– essen
an	egg	– ein Ei
	electrical	– elektrisch
	electricity	– Elektrizität
	electrics	– Elektrik
	elegant	– elegant
	energy	– Energie
	English	– englisch
to	enjoy	– genießen
	enjoy your meal	– Genieß(t) dein/ euer Essen, Guten Appetit
	enough	– genug, ausreichend
an	entertainment	– eine Unterhaltung, Zerstreuung
	equal	– gleich
	equality	– Gleichberechtigung
an	equipment	– eine Ausrüstung
an	evening	– ein Abend
	every	– jede, jeder, jedes
	everybody	– alle
	everybody	– jeder
	everywhere	– überall
to	examine	– untersuchen
	excited	– aufgeregt
an	exercise book	– ein Schreibheft
	expensive	– teuer
an	experience	– eine Erfahrung
an	expert	– ein Experte
to	express	– sich ausdrücken
	extremely	– extrem

F

a	face	– ein Gesicht
a	facial expression	– ein Gesichtsausdruck
to	fall	– fallen
a	family	– eine Familie
	famous	– berühmt
a	fancy dress costume	– ein Kostüm
	fantastic	– fantastisch
	far	– weit
	fast	– schnell
a	father	– ein Vater
	favourite	– Lieblings …
	favourite (food)	– Lieblings... (-essen)
	February	– Februar
to	feel	– fühlen
to	feel ill	– sich krank fühlen
a	felt-tip	– ein Filzstift
a	fence	– ein Zaun
	fever	– Fieber
a	few	– einige, wenige
a	field	– ein Feld
to	fight	– kämpfen
to	fight against someone/ something	– gegen jemanden/ etwas kämpfen
to	fight for something	– um etwas kämpfen
to	fill in (the grid)	– (Raster) ausfüllen
a	final	– ein Finale
	financial	– finanziell

to	find	– finden
a	finish	– ein Ziel (Spiel)
to	finish	– beenden
	first	– erst, erstens, erste, erster
the	first	– der, die, das erste
a	fish	– ein Fisch
	five	– fünf
a	flea market	– ein Flohmarkt
a	flower	– eine Blume
the	flu	– die Grippe
to	fold	– falten
	food	– Essen, Nahrungsmittel
a	football	– ein Fußball
	for	– für
	for sure	– sicher, selbstverständlich
to	forget	– vergessen
a	fork	– eine Gabel
	fortunately	– günstiger Weise
	forward	– vorwärts
	four	– vier
the	fourth	– der, die, das vierte
	French Fries	– Pommes Frites
	fresh	– frisch
	Friday	– Freitag
on	Fridays	– freitags
a	friend	– ein Freund, eine Freundin
	friendly	– freundlich
at	friends	– bei Freunden
a	friendship	– eine Freundschaft
	from	– von
a	fruit	– eine Frucht
	fruit	– Obst
	fun	– Spaß
	funny	– lustig
	furniture	– Möbel
	further	– weiter

G

a	game	– ein Spiel
a	game piece	– Spielstein
a	gap	– eine Lücke
	gardening	– Gartenarbeiten
to	gather	– versammeln, sammeln
a	germ	– ein Keim
	Germany	– Deutschland
to	get	– bekommen
to	get along with something	– mit etwas zurechtkommen
to	get dirty	– schmutzig werden
to	get home	– nach Hause kommen
to	get on	– einsteigen
to	get up	– aufstehen
	get well soon	– Gute Besserung
a	giant	– ein Riese
a	girl	– ein Mädchen
a	girlfriend	– Freundin (Liebesbeziehung)
to	give	– geben
a	glass	– ein Glas
to	go	– gehen
to	go shopping	– einkaufen gehen
to	go with	– einhergehen mit (passen)
	good	– gut, gute
	good and bad times	– gute und schlechte Zeiten
to	grate	– reiben
a	grave	– ein Grab
	gravy	– Soße
	great	– großartig, prima, toll
	groceries	– Lebensmittel
to	grow up	– aufwachsen

to	guess	– raten
a	guest	– ein Gast

H

a	habit	– eine (An)gewohnheit
	hair	– Haare
a	half	– eine Hälfte
	ham	– Schinken
a	hand	– eine Hand
to	hang out	– abhängen
to	happen	– passieren
	hard	– schwierig, anstrengend, hart
	harvest time	– Erntezeit
a	hat	– ein Hut
to	hate	– hassen
to	have	– haben
to	have a look	– nachschauen, anschauen
to	have a temperature	– Fieber haben
	he	– er
a	head	– ein Kopf
to	head for something	– auf etwas zusteuern
a	headache	– Kopfschmerzen
a	headline	– eine Schlagzeile
	healthy	– gesund
to	help	– helfen
	her	– ihr
	here	– hier
	hi	– hallo
	high	– hoch
	higher	– höher
the	highest	– der, die, das höchste
	him	– ihn/ihm
	his	– sein
	his	– sein/seine
	hockey	– Hockey
a	hole	– ein Loch
a	holiday	– ein Urlaub
a	home	– ein Zuhause
at	home	– zu Hause
	honey	– Honig
a	hotel	– ein Hotel
a	house	– ein Haus
	House of Commons	– Unterhaus des britischen Parlaments
	House of Lords	– Oberhaus des britischen Parlaments
the	Houses of Parliament	– das Parlamentsgebäude (britischer Regierungssitz)
	how	– wie
	how about (this DVD?)	– Wie wär's mit (dieser DVD?)
	how much	– wie viel
	hungry	– hungrig
to	hunt	– jagen

I

	I	– ich
	I'm = I am	– Ich bin
an	ice cube	– ein Eiswürfel
an	ice-cream	– Eis
an	idea	– eine Idee
	identification	– Identifikation
to	identify	– erkennen, identifizieren
	if	– falls, wenn, ob
to	imagine	– sich denken, sich etwas vorstellen
	importance	– Bedeutung, Wichtigkeit
	important	– wichtig
	impressed	– beeindruckt
	in	– in

	in pairs	– zu zweit
	in the end	– am Ende
	in the evening	– am Abend
	in the front	– vorne
	in the middle	– in der Mitte
	incorrect	– fehlerhaft
	incredible	– unglaublich
an	infection	– eine Infektionskrankheit
to	inform	– informieren
an	information	– eine Information
an	information center	– ein Informationszentrum
to	install	– installieren, einrichten
an	instruction	– eine Anweisung
an	interest	– ein Interesse
	interesting	– interessant
an	interview partner	– ein Interviewpartner
to	interview someone	– jemanden interviewen
	into	– in … hinein
to	invent	– erfinden
an	invitation card	– eine Einladungskarte
to	invite	– einladen
	is	– ist
	is going to	– wird (in der Zukunft)
	it	– es
	it's = it is	– es ist

J

	January	– Januar
	jelly	– Gelee
a	job	– ein Job, eine Arbeit
	juice	– Saft
	July	– Juli
	June	– Juni
	just	– gerade eben

K

to	keep something a secret	– etwas geheim halten
to	kill	– töten, umbringen
a	kind	– eine Art, eine Sorte
a	kiss	– ein Kuss
a	kitchen	– eine Küche
a	knee	– ein Knie
a	knife	– ein Messer
to	know	– wissen

L

a	ladyfinger	– ein Löffelbiskuit
a	lamp	– eine Lampe
a	language	– eine Sprache
	large	– groß
the	last	– der/die/das Letzte
	later	– später
to	laugh	– lachen
to	laugh at someone	– jemanden auslachen
to	lay	– (etwas) legen
to	learn	– lernen
to	leave	– verlassen
	left	– links
a	legend	– eine Legende
	less	– weniger
	less than	– weniger als
	let's (let us)	– lass uns
a	letter	– ein Buchstabe
a	library	– eine Bibliothek
a	lie	– eine Lüge
a	life	– ein Leben

to	light	– erleuchten
a	light (lights)	– ein Licht (Lichter)
	light	– leicht (Gewicht)
	like	– wie (im Vergleich)
to	like	– mögen
a	limit	– ein Limit, eine Grenze
a	line	– eine Linie
a	line	– eine Linie (eines Bus- oder U-Bahnfahrplanes)
a	list	– eine Liste
to	listen to	– zuhören
	little	– klein
a	little	– ein wenig
a	little bit	– ein bisschen
to	live	– leben
a	living room	– ein Wohnzimmer
	loads and loads	– eine große Menge
	logical	– logisch
	long	– lang
to	look	– schauen, sehen, aussehen
to	look at something	– etwas anschauen
to	look cool	– cool aussehen
to	look for something	– etwas suchen
to	look funny	– lustig aussehen
to	look good	– gut aussehen
to	look something up	– etwas nachschlagen
the	looks	– das Aussehen
	looks of hair	– Aussehen der Haare
to	lose	– verlieren
a	lot	– eine Menge, viel
a	lot (of)	– viel (von)
a	lot of	– viele
	lots of	– viele

	loud	– laut
	love	– Liebe
to	love	– lieben, etwas sehr mögen
	lovely	– lieblich, zum lieb haben
a	lover	– ein/-e Geliebte/-r
a	luck	– ein Glück
	lucky	– Glück haben
to	be lucky	– glücklich sein
	lyrics	– Liedertext

M

to	make	– machen
to	make a plan	– einen Plan machen
to	make someone laugh	– jemanden zum Lachen bringen
a	man	– ein Mann
	many	– viele
a	march	– Demonstration
	March	– März
to	mark	– markieren
	mashed potatoes	– Kartoffelbrei,-püree
to	match	– verbinden, zuordnen
	May	– Mai
	me	– mir
a	meal	– eine Mahlzeit
a	meaning	– eine Bedeutung
	meat	– Fleisch
a	mechanic	– ein Mechaniker
	medicine	– Medizin
to	meet	– treffen
to	meet someone	– jemanden treffen
	met	– traf (Vergangenheit von „to meet“)
a	microphone	– ein Mikrofon

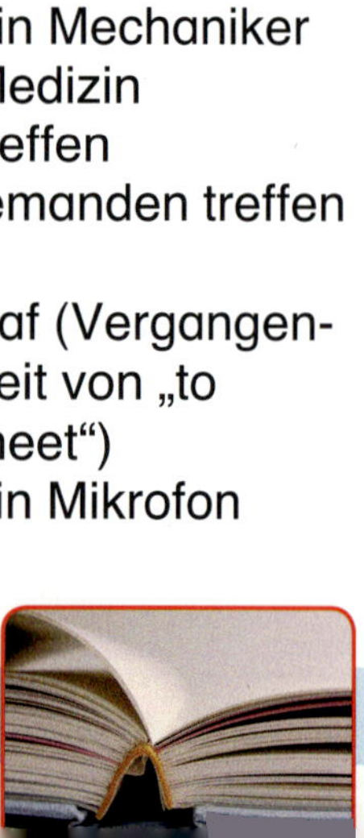

a	microwave oven	– ein Mikrowellenherd
the	middle	– in der Mitte
a	middle	– eine Mitte
	milk	– Milch
the	mind	– der Sinn
a	mind	– ein Verstand
a	mind map	– eine „Gedankenkarte“
	mineral water	– Mineralwasser
a	minute	– eine Minute
to	miss	– fehlen, verfehlen, verpassen
to	mix	– (ver)mischen
a	mixer	– ein Mixer
	Monday	– Montag
the	money	– das Geld
a	monitor	– ein Monitor, Bildschirm
a	month	– ein Monat
	more	– mehr
	more than	– mehr als
	most	– am meisten
a	mother	– eine Mutter
to	move	– umziehen, rücken, bewegen
	much	– viel
	multiple choice	– Multiple choice (Prüfungsverfahren, aus mehreren zur Verfügung stehenden Antworten muss die richtige herausgefunden werden)
a	mum	– eine Mama, eine Mutter
	music	– Musik
a	musician	– ein Musiker
	must	– müssen
	mustn't	– nicht dürfen
	my	– mein, meine, meins
	myself	– ich, mir selbst

N

to	name	– benennen
a	name	– ein Name
to be	named	– benannt werden, benannt sein
a	national holiday	– ein nationaler Feiertag
a	native American	– ein/-e Indianer/-in
	natural	– natürlich, aus der Natur
a	necklace	– eine Kette
to	need	– brauchen, benötigen
a	needle	– eine Nadel
	needn't	– nicht müssen
	negative	– negativ
a	neighbour	– ein Nachbar
	new	– neu
	New Year's Day	– Neujahrstag
a	news	– eine Nachricht
a	newspaper	– eine Zeitung
a	newsreader	– ein Nachrichtensprecher
	next	– nächste, nächster, nächstes
	nice	– nett, schön
	no	– nein
	No way!	– Auf keinen Fall!
to	nominate	– nominieren
	not	– nicht
	not anymore	– nicht mehr
	not yet	– noch nicht
to	note	– Notizen machen
a	note	– eine Note, eine Notiz

	November	– November
	now	– jetzt, nun
	nowadays	– heutzutage
a	number	– eine Nummer

O

	o'clock	– Uhr
	October	– Oktober
	oil	– Öl
	old	– alt
	on	– auf
	on the phone	– am Telefon
	one	– eins
	ones	– eigene, eigenes
	only	– nur
	onto	– auf … drauf
an	opinion	– eine Meinung
	or	– oder
	orange juice	– Orangensaft
to	order	– bestellen
an	order	– die Reihenfolge
an	ordinal number	– eine Ordinalzahl
to	organize	– organisieren
	other	– andere, anderer, anderes
	our	– unser, unsere
	outside	– draußen
	over	– über
	own	– eigene, eigenes

P

a	page	– eine Seite
to	paint	– malen, anmalen, streichen
a	pair of jeans	– eine Jeanshose
a	paper	– ein Papier
a	paper tissue	– Papiertaschentuch
a	paperclip	– eine Büroklammer
	parents	– die Eltern
a	park	– ein Park
	parmesan cheese	– Parmesan(-käse)
a	part	– ein Teil, ein Teilbereich
a	partner	– ein Partner
to	party	– feiern
	party	– eine Party
to	pass	– herübergeben, weitergeben, passieren, vorbeigehen, vorbeikommen
to	pass something to someone	– jemandem etwas geben
a	patient	– ein Patient
to	pay	– bezahlen
a	pea	– eine Erbse
	peaceful	– gewaltfrei, friedlich
a	peach	– ein Pfirsich
	peanut butter	– Erdnussbutter
a	pear	– eine Birne
to	peel	– schälen
the	people	– die Leute
	people	– Personen, Menschen
	pepper	– Pfeffer
	per (day)	– pro (Tag)
	perfect	– perfekt
a	phone (telephone)	– ein Telefon
a	photograph	– ein Foto
a	piano	– ein Klavier
a	picture	– ein Bild
a	pie	– ein Kuchen
a	piece	– ein Stück
a	piggy bank	– ein Sparschwein

a	Pilgrim	– ein Pilger
a	pineapple	– Ananas
	pineapple juice	– Ananassaft
a	pizza	– eine Pizza
to	place	– (hin)stellen
a	place	– ein Ort
a	plan	– ein Plan
to	plan	– planen
to	plant	– pflanzen
a	plate	– ein Teller
to	play	– spielen
to	play cards	– Karten spielen
	please	– bitte
the	pocket money	– das Taschengeld
a	poem	– ein Gedicht
a	point	– ein Punkt
	poor	– arm
	popular	– bekannt
	positive	– positiv
a	possibility	– eine Möglichkeit
	possible	– möglich
a	poster	– ein Poster
a	potato (pl. potatoes)	– eine Kartoffel (Kartoffeln)
to	pour	– gießen
a	preparation	– eine Vorbereitung
to	prepare	– vorbereiten
a	present	– ein Geschenk
to	present something	– etwas präsentieren
	Prime Minister	– Premierminister
a	print	– ein Ausdruck (z. B. aus einem Drucker)
to	print	– drucken
a	prize	– ein Preis
	pro	– für (etwas sein)
	probably	– wahrscheinlich
a	problem	– ein Problem
to	propose	– vorschlagen
a	psychological test	– ein psychologischer Test
a	pullover	– ein Pullover
a	pupil's book	– ein Schülerbuch
to	put	– setzen
to	put up	– aufhängen
a	puzzle	– ein Puzzle

Q

a	question	– eine Frage
to	quit with something	– mit etwas aufhören

R

a	ranking list	– eine Rangliste
	Ravioli	– Ravioli (gefüllte Nudeltaschen)
to	reach	– erreichen
to	read	– lesen
	ready	– bereit
	ready-made custard	– ein Fertig-Vanillepudding
	really	– wirklich
a	reason	– ein Grund
a	receptionist	– Sprechstundenhilfe
a	recipe	– ein Rezept zum Kochen
a	refreshment	– eine Erfrischung, Stärkung
a	refrigerator	– ein Kühlschrank
to	relax	– entspannen
to	remember	– (sich) erinnern
to	repair	– reparieren
to	repeat	– wiederholen
to	replace	– ersetzen

a	replica	– eine Reproduktion, ein Replikat, ein Nachbau
a	report	– ein Bericht
to	report	– berichten
a	reporter	– ein Reporter, ein Berichterstatter
a	resource	– ein Mittel
to	rest	– sich ausruhen
a	restaurant	– ein Restaurant
to	rewrite	– neu schreiben, umschreiben
	rice	– Reis
	rich	– reich
to	ride	– reiten
	right	– rechts
	rights	– Rechte
	roast beef	– Rinderbraten, Roastbeef
to	rob	– ausrauben
a	robot	– ein Roboter
a	role	– eine Rolle
a	rose	– eine Rose
a	rule	– eine Spielregel, ein Gesetz
to	rule	– regeln
a	ruler	– ein Lineal

S

	sad	– traurig
to	sail	– segeln
a	salad	– ein Salat
	salt	– Salz
	same	– dasselbe, derselbe, dieselbe
a	sandwich	– ein Sandwich
	Saturday	– Samstag
a	sausage	– eine Wurst
to	save	– sparen
the	saving	– das Ersparte
to	say	– sagen
a	school	– eine Schule
at	school	– in der Schule
a	schoolmate	– Schulkamerad/-in, Klassenkamerad/-in
	scissors	– eine Schere
a	screwdriver	– ein Schraubendreher
a	seat	– ein Sitz
the	second	– der, die, das zweite
a	secret	– ein Geheimnis
to	see	– sehen
to	sell	– verkaufen
a	sentence	– ein Satz
	September	– September
a	servant	– ein/-e Diener/-in
to	serve	– servieren
to	set on fire	– anzünden
to	set the table	– den Tisch decken
to	sew	– nähen
to	shine	– scheinen, leuchten
a	ship	– ein Schiff
a	shoe	– ein Schuh
a	shoe box	– ein Schuhkarton
a	shop	– ein Laden
	should	– sollte
to	show	– zeigen
	sightseeing	– Besichtigung von Sehenswürdigkeiten
	similar	– ähnlich
to	sing	– singen
a	singer	– ein Sänger, eine Sängerin
a	sister	– eine Schwester
to	sit (around)	– (herum-)sitzen
	skin	– Haut
the	sleep	– der Schlaf
to	sleep	– schlafen

	slept	– schlief (Vergangenheit von „to sleep“)
to	slice	– in Scheiben schneiden
a	slice of bread	– eine Brotscheibe
	small	– klein
	smart	– schlau
to	smile	– lächeln
a	snack	– ein Imbiss, ein Snack
	so	– so
	some	– einige
	something	– etwas
	sometimes	– manchmal
a	song	– ein Lied
a	sore throat	– Halsschmerzen
	sour cream	– saure Sahne
a	souvenir	– ein Souvenir, ein Erinnerungsstück, ein Andenken
to	speak	– sprechen
	special	– besonders, besonderer, besonderes
a	speech bubble	– eine Sprechblase
to	spell	– richtig schreiben (eigentl.: orthographisch richtig schreiben)
	spoke	– sprach (Vergangenheit von „to speak“)
a	spoon	– ein Löffel
to	spoon	– löffeln
	spring	– Frühling
a	spring onion	– eine Frühlingszwiebel
a	square	– ein Viereck, Quadrat
a	staircase	– eine Treppe
to	stand up	– aufstehen
to	stand up for someone	– sich für jemanden einsetzen
	start	– Start (Spiel)
a	statement	– eine Meinung, eine Aussage
a	station	– eine Station, eine Haltestelle
to	stay	– bleiben
to	stay at home	– zu Hause bleiben
a	step	– ein Schritt
a	stereo system	– eine Stereoanlage
to	stick	– kleben
	still	– (immer) noch
	stomach	– Bauch
a	stomach ache	– Bauchschmerzen
to	stop	– halten
a	story	– eine Geschichte
	strange	– merkwürdig, eigenartig
a	street	– eine Straße
a	stuffed turkey	– ein gefüllter Truthahn
a	style	– ein Aussehen
a	subject	– ein Thema
	such	– solch, solche, solches
	suddenly	– plötzlich
	sugar	– Zucker
to	suggest	– vorschlagen
a	suggestion	– ein Vorschlag
to	summarise	– zusammenfassen
a	summary	– eine Zusammenfassung
	superficial	– oberflächlich
a	supermarket	– ein Supermarkt
	sure	– sicher
a	surgery	– Arztpraxis

to	swap	– tauschen
	sweet	– süß
a	sweet pepper	– eine Paprika
	sweets	– Süßigkeiten
to	swim	– schwimmen
to	switch	– schalten
a	switch	– ein Schalter

T

a	table	– ein Tisch, eine Tabelle
	table football	– Kicker
	table tennis	– Tischtennis
a	tablet	– eine Tablette
to	take	– nehmen
to	take an X-ray	– röntgen
to	take care of someone	– sich um jemanden kümmern
to	take the temperature	– Fieber messen
to	talk	– reden, sprechen, sich unterhalten
to	taste	– schmecken
	taught	– unterrichtete, lehrte (Vergangenheit von „to teach")
a	taxi	– ein Taxi
to	teach	– unterrichten, beibringen
a	teacher	– ein/-e Lehrer/-in
a	team	– ein Team
a	teaspoon	– ein Teelöffel
a	teen	– ein Teenager, Jugendlicher
a	television	– ein Fernseher, ein Fernsehgerät

to	tell	– mitteilen, erzählen, sagen
a	temperature	– eine Temperatur, auch: Fieber
	tennis	– Tennis
	terrible	– schrecklich, furchtbar
a	text	– ein Text
a	textbook	– ein Lesebuch
	than	– als (im Vergleich)
	thank you	– danke
	that	– das
	the	– der, die, das
	their	– ihr, ihre (Besitz)
	them	– ihnen
	then	– dann
	There you go!	– Bitte sehr!
a	thermometer	– ein Thermometer
	these	– diese
	they	– sie (3. Person Plural)
a	thing	– ein Ding, eine Sache
to	think	– denken
the	third	– der, die, das dritte
	this	– diese, dieser, dieses
a	thought	– ein Gedanke
a	thread	– ein Faden
to	throw	– werfen
	Thursday	– Donnerstag
to	tick	– abhaken
to	tick	– ankreuzen
	time	– Zeit
the	time	– die Zeit
to	tire	– ermüden
a	title	– ein Titel
a	toaster	– ein Toaster
	today	– heute
	together	– zusammen

a tomato (pl.: tomatoes) – eine Tomate
tomorrow – morgen
too – auch
took – nahm (Vergangenheit von „to take“)
on top of something – auf etwas drauf
a topic – eine Überschrift
a topping – Garnierung
a tourist – ein Tourist, eine Touristin
a tower – ein Turm
a travel – eine Reise
to travel – reisen
a tray – ein Tablett
a treatment – eine Behandlung
a trifle – ein englischer Nachtisch
trouble – Schwierigkeiten
to try – versuchen
a tube – eine Tube
the tube – Begriff für die Londoner U-Bahn
to turn around – sich umdrehen
twice – zweimal
two – zwei
a type – ein Typ
a type of – eine Art von
typical – typisch

U

ugly – hässlich
an underground – eine U-Bahn (allgemeiner Begriff)
unfortunately – unglücklicher Weise
until – bis
USA (United States of America) – USA (Die vereinigten Staaten von Amerika)
to use – brauchen, verwenden, benutzen

V

a Valentine’s card – eine Valentinskarte
vanilla – Vanille
a vase – eine Vase
vegetable – Gemüse
a verb – ein Verb, ein Tätigkeitswort
very – sehr
violent – gewaltsam
a visit – ein Besuch
to visit – besuchen
vitamins – Vitamine
voting rights – Wahlrecht

W

to wait – warten
a waiting room – ein Wartezimmer
to wake up – aufwachen
to walk – laufen, spazieren gehen
a wall – die Wand
to want – wollen
war – Krieg
warm – warm
was/were – war (Vergangenheit von „to be“)
to wash – waschen
to watch – anschauen, gucken, beobachten

a	watch	– eine Armbanduhr
	water	– Wasser
a	way	– ein Weg
	we	– wir
to	wear	– tragen
a	weather	– ein Wetter
a	week	– eine Woche
	well	– gut
	Wembley	– Fußballstadion in London
	went	– ging (Vergangenheit von „to go“)
	were	– waren (Vergangenheit von „to be“)
	what	– was
	what for	– wofür
	what kind of	– welche Art
	when	– wann, wenn, als
	where	– wo
	which	– welche, welcher, welches
	whipped cream	– Schlagsahne
to	whisper	– flüstern
	white people	– Weiße
	who	– wer
	whole	– ganze, ganzes, ganzer
	why	– warum
a	window	– ein Fenster
to	window-shop	– Schaufenster bummeln
a	winner	– ein Gewinner
	winter	– Winter
a	witch	– eine Hexe
	with	– mit
	with each other	– miteinander
	wonderful	– wunderbar
a	word list	– eine Wortliste
a	word picture	– ein Wortbild
	wore	– trug (Vergangenheit von „to wear“)
to	work	– arbeiten
to	work something out	– etwas ausarbeiten
	World Cup	– Weltmeistertrophäe
	would	– würde
to	write	– schreiben
to	write something down	– etwas aufschreiben
	wrong	– falsch
	wrote	– schrieb (Vergangenheit von „to write“)

X

an	X-ray	– ein Röntgenbild

Y

a	year	– ein Jahr
	yes	– ja
	yesterday	– gestern
	yoga	– Yoga
	you	– du, ihr
	you'll = you will	– du wirst, ihr werdet (in der Zukunft)
	You're doing well!	– Das machst du gut!
	young	– jung
	your	– dein, deine
	your own	– dein eigenes, deine eigenen
a	youth club	– ein Jugendclub
a	youth hostel	– eine Jugendherberge

Beginn und Ende	
Good morning. How are you?	Guten Morgen. Wie geht es dir/euch/ Ihnen?
Good bye. See you tomorrow.	Auf Wiedersehen. Bis morgen.
Fragen	
Can you help me?	Kannst du mir/Können Sie mir helfen?
What's „Freunde treffen“ in English?	Was heißt „Freunde treffen“ auf Englisch?
What's „meeting friends“ in German?	Was heißt “meeting friends” auf Deutsch?
Could you say that again?	Kannst du/Können Sie das wieder-holen?
Can I borrow your ruler?	Kann ich mir dein/Ihr Lineal auslei-hen?
Can I go to the toilet?	Darf ich zur Toilette gehen?
Arbeitsanweisungen	
Listen to the CD, please.	Höre dir/Hört euch die CD an.
Match the words and the pictures.	Ordne/ordnet die Wörter den Bildern zu.
You need a pencil/ruler.	Du/Ihr braucht einen Bleistift/ein Lineal.
Hold an interview.	Führe/Führt ein Interview durch.
Let's make a list.	Lasst uns eine Liste machen.
Open your books on page …, please.	Schlagt bitte eure Bücher auf Seite ... auf.
Work with a partner.	Arbeitet mit einem Partner.
Work in teams of four.	Arbeitet zu viert.
Write down your answers.	Schreibt eure Antworten auf.
Act the scene.	Spiele/Spielt es vor.
Come to the board, please.	Komme bitte an die Tafel.
Come and sit in a circle.	Kommt her und macht einen Sitzkreis.

Lob, Ermahnung und Dank	
That's right. Very good. Well done.	Das ist richtig. Sehr gut. Gut gemacht.
Attention, please. Listen to me.	Ich bitte um Aufmerksamkeit. Hört mir zu.
Be quiet, please.	Bitte seid leise.
Thank you. Thank you very much.	Danke. Vielen Dank.
Entschuldigung	
Sorry, I'm late.	Entschuldigen Sie die Verspätung.
Sorry, I don't have my book/my homework/my pencil.	Entschuldigung, ich habe mein Buch/meine Hausaufgaben/meinen Bleistift nicht.

Do you remember?

Track 01
(see page 8)

Paul: "Hey, that was fun! Do you remember? In this picture we were at the mirror cabinet. You looked funny."

Emily: "You looked funny, too. And here, that was our first day at school. We put up posters on the wall."

Paul: "Yes, and we met all our new friends for the first time. Look, here you can see Robin. That was when we talked about the new colour of the classroom."

Emily: "Yes, we painted it blue in the end."

Paul: "Oh, Emily, look! This is an old photo of Teddy. He was so small. Now he's much bigger."

Emily: "Yes, but he's still cute. And that was at Christmas last year. We decorated your Christmas tree. Your parents were so busy."

Paul: "Yes, but we moved into this house not long before that. Here's a picture. I'm in front of our new house."

Emily: "It's a nice house. And it's close to the underground station and to our school. Here, that was when we went into town that one day and took the underground."

Paul: "Oh, yes. We went to the music shop and had an ice-cream later. I still like the CD."

Emily: "Can't you play it? I like to hear it. Oh wait, here's one last picture. – Oh, that was when I couldn't find my maths folder."

Paul: "Did you find it in the end?"

Emily: "Yes, I did. It was right in front of me on the table. I was so blind!"

At the doctor's

Track 26
(see page 48)

Doctor: "Hello Emily."
Emily: "Hello Doctor. I feel really ill."
Doctor: "What is the problem?"
Emily: "I've got a sore throat. My head aches and I've got a fever."
Doctor: "I must examine you. Let me see. Open your mouth."
Emily: "– Aaaa –"
Doctor: "OK, now I must take your temperature."
Emily: "Is it bad?"
Doctor: "No, it isn't bad. You've got the flu. But you mustn't go to school for five days and you must take this medicine."
Emily: "OK, doctor. Thank you."
Doctor: "No problem. Get well soon! Bye."

Bildquellenverzeichnis

© Fotolia.com: S. 40/o. l. (Beboy), 40/o. M. (volff), 40/o. r. (Lucky Dragon), 40/M. l. (angelo.gi), 40/M. r. (angelo.gi), 40/u. (Simone van den Berg), 41/o. l. (sun_orbiter), 41/2. v. r. (Dušan Zidar), 41/u. (felix), 58/M. (ChristianSchwier.de), 58/u. (Franz Pfluegl), 61/o. (Maria.P.), 61/2. v. o. (Lianem), 61/M. (Franz Pfluegl), 61/u. (Horticulture), 76/u. l. (sheldon gardner), 77/u. r. (L. Shat), 85 (Edyta Pawlowska), 91 (Joe Gough); MEV Verlags GmbH, Augsburg: S. 41/2. v. l., 41/o. r., 58/o., 61/2. v. u., 99/o. l., 99/o. M., 99/M. l., 99/M. r., 99/u. r.; Patterson, Kevin Marc: S. 76/o. l., 76/M., 77/o. r; Picture-alliance: S. 39, 84, 94, 99/o. r., 99/M. M., 99/u. l., 99/u. M., 105; Sutter, Anne: S. 25; mauritius images: Umschlagfoto; Grafiken: Pohle, Marlene (außer S. 27/r., 68/u., 69/u., 82, 83); Bergt, Raimo (S. 6/Karten, 7/Karten, 68/u., 69/u.); Brauner, Angelika (S. 82, 83); Galas, Elisabeth (S. 27/r.)

Textquellenverzeichnis

McTell, Ralph, Streets of London, by Westminster Music Ltd, D/A/CH: Essex Musikvertrieb GmbH, Hamburg: S. 84; Lennon, John/McCartney, Paul, A day in the life, Maclen Joint Ltd./ Northern Songs Ltd., EMI Music Publishing Germany GmbH & Co. KG, Hamburg, Sony/ATV Music Publishing (Germany) GmbH, Berlin: S. 94